Praise for *Logosynthesis*

Willem Lammers has written a thought-provoking meld of mind, body, and Essence. He theorises that life events can mar, distort, and disrupt our true way of being, resulting in suffering. This well-written and easy to read self-guide spells out steps to foster reconnection with our true living Self while fostering knowledge and self-stabilisation.

'Practical' and 'powerful' best define Logosynthesis, and this is a must read for those wanting to promote a betterment of life and living.

John H. Diepold, Jr., Ph.D., DCEP, Licensed Psychologist
Co-author of *Evolving Thought Field Therapy*
Originator and author, Heart-Assisted Therapy

Dr. Lammers welcomes you to the 'world behind the mirror,' drawing upon sophisticated psychological principles and methods for discovering your Essence. As conventional psychiatry strays from the world of psyche and spirit, Logosynthesis is a welcome, creative contribution for bringing us back to the core of who we are, opening a door to greater happiness, fulfilment, and inner peace.

David Feinstein, Ph.D.
Co-author of *Personal Mythology*

Logosynthesis is a breakthrough technique for self-healing that is easy to do, effective, and uncomplicated. Unlike Talk Therapy, this streamlined method invokes positive change rapidly and permanently. Once you learn Logosynthesis you can use it anytime and anywhere to deal with fears, stress, anxiety and other life issues.

Gloria Arenson, MFT, DCEP

A comprehensive and well-written handbook for counsellors, coaches, and therapists outlining how to use this fascinating new approach to guided change to produce transformative changes for yourself and your clients. Innovative, user-friendly, and deceptively simple, Logosynthesis uses the power of words to create powerful personal changes. The method empowers ordinary people to use their own intention to resolve upsetting emotional problems and achieve their life goals, and offers therapists, counsellors, and coaches a powerful set of change tools that really work.

This handbook incorporates many refinements and improvements gained through clinical experiences, and shows the depth to which the author has gone in exploring how to maximise results for practitioners and help them better help their clients. It clearly outlines the assumptions and philosophy behind the method and offers a comprehensive outline with clear explanations on how to treat various conditions most effectively. It also includes many revealing case examples and transcripts from sessions with real clients to illustrate the many and varied applications of Logosynthesis in counselling, coaching, and therapy.

Practitioners will find this a valued resource that they will return to time and again to draw from its wisdom and learn from its many helpful distinctions on ways to better help their clients to return their energy to flow and achieve their life tasks.

Highly recommended for anyone who is interested in learning this innovative method to empower their clients to create profound changes.

Steve Wells
Psychologist and Peak Performance Consultant
Co-author of *Enjoy Emotional Freedom*
Co-creator of Simple Energy Techniques (SET)

WILLEM LAMMERS

Logosynthesis – Healing with Words

WILLEM LAMMERS

LOGOSYNTHESIS – HEALING WITH WORDS

A Handbook for the Helping Professions
with a Preface by Dr. Fred Gallo

For my companions on the journey

Contents

III Logosynthesis live: a glance over my shoulder

IV Applying Logosynthesis

V In conclusion

Foreword

In the beginning was the Word,
and the Word was with God,
and the Word was God.

--GOSPEL OF JOHN 1:1

PERHAPS AS MANY AS SEVEN MILLENNIA AGO THE IDEA EMERGED THAT OUR BODIES POSSESS VARIOUS INTRICATE ENERGY SYSTEMS. We can only speculate as to how these inspirations arose, but increasing evidence abounds that the ancients were correct. This understanding has been basic to physics for some time now. This and related understandings gave birth to meridian and chakra therapies, yoga, meditation, and more. However the understanding is even deeper than this, since it appears that at core we *are* the energy.

Logosynthesis is the brainchild of my friend, colleague, and noted Swiss psychologist and psychotherapist, Dr. Willem Lammers. Willem and I met in the early days of energy psychology. At that time our primary treatment approach involved promoting the flow of blocked energy through meridians to efficiently treat psychological problems. Basically we tapped. And the tapping was often accompanied by affirmation, specific body postures, muscle testing, and more. Although approaches based on these concepts and procedures are highly effective, most of us who have travelled this path discovered other ways to effect profound and often instant healing. Many of us have become interested in mindfulness as well as bodily and other energy systems in the treatment process, and as a result we have developed a deep understanding of life. Our methods have evolved. And this is precisely what Willem has accomplished by mindfully harvesting the power of intention and words to release energy blocked in time and space, and thus help people to get in touch with their core Self, their true Essence.

It is very interesting to me that at core we do not suffer; we are immutable. Rather suffering occurs in blocked energy and a split from our true Self. In actuality it's not that we have an Essence, but rather that we are the Essence. Long ago in many primal cultures this was the common understanding. Then, after a number of devastating wars, a nihilistic view set in that turned things upside-down and some cultures concluded that we have no Essence prior to existence. It was a hopeless time in our history. The shaman would observe that the soul was split off or fragmented and retrieval was in order. Logosynthesis is in good company with this understanding and mission.

So now we return to the deep understanding that at core we are spiritual beings and Essence. True we have bodies and we are bodies in one dimension. But we are many dimensions, and at core we are eternal. Logosynthesis is based on and leads to this awareness as the power of words makes healing wonderfully accessible.

In the beginning there was the Word, and the Word is the way to new beginnings. As you read this book and apply its magic, I wish you well, words of freedom, and happy new beginnings.

Fred P. Gallo, PhD
Author of *Energy Psychology*

Preface:
make it simple

If you can't make it simple,
you don't understand it well enough.

--ALBERT EINSTEIN

LENORE LOOKED AT ME WITH WIDE, FRIGHTENED EYES. She had just told me how she had tried to leave her shower that morning but had missed the cubicle door and repeatedly felt her hand grab at the glass instead. Experiences like this were becoming common and she was feeling confused and desperate. She summarised her situation with a phrase in her native Swiss German that means 'I'm crazy' – but literally translates as; 'I'm standing beside my shoes.'

I intuitively took her phrase literally and asked her to move back into her shoes, into the right place. I don't know how she did it, but she suddenly became aware of pictures; she recalled falling down the stairs in a freezing train station and being injured. The accident had happened early in the morning six years before.

My session with Leonore took place on 11 January 2005. The meeting challenged me as an expert. How could I understand what had happened? Logosynthesis is my answer to this question. It's a versatile new approach to the relief of human suffering; a comprehensive, elegant, and effective system for both guided and self-coached change.

This book is a sequel to my 2008 book *Logosynthesis – Once you hit the magic word*. I've learnt a lot since I wrote that book, and Logosynthesis has been refined and made simpler to understand. My first years of working with the model were hindered by my training and experience as a psychologist, psychotherapist, and coach. I tried to anchor Logosynthesis in broadly traditional schools of counselling and psychotherapy – psychoanalysis, transactional analysis, hypnotherapy, NLP, EMDR, and energy psychology. I've since come to understand that relying on existing knowledge can limit your understanding of Logosynthesis. I've gradually given up many cherished convictions since that day in January years ago.

The book deals with Logosynthesis' new, simpler form in the context of guided change. I use the generic term 'guided change' as the model supports professionals from a wide range of coaching, counselling, psychotherapy, and supervision approaches. Simplification efforts have also extended to self-coaching with Logosynthesis; the eBook *Restoring the Flow: A Primer in Logosynthesis*[1], written with Andrea Fredi, is a guide to self-application of the model. It contains answers to some of the most frequently asked questions in self-coaching, and it's an excellent introduction and supplement to the information that's contained within this book.

It's important to read the upcoming chapters with a sense of curiosity. Read the book as science fiction if you're sceptical, perhaps considering Logosynthesis as a thought experiment for a future world. Then try out the model. You may not share my basic assumptions, but I can assure you that the methods that I describe apply exactly as I describe them. Get to know Logosynthesis and gain experience with the healing power of words.

---

[1] Lammers, W. & Fredi, A. (2012). Restoring the Flow – a Primer of Logosynthesis. URL: https://www.smashwords.com/books/view/284465. Retrieved 6 May 2014.

I still continue to be fascinated by Logosynthesis' potential for my clients, for my colleagues, and for myself. My experience shows that the approach is successful as both a model and a method – giving me confidence that we're working with an immense truth.

How will you read this book?

Fewer and fewer people read books from cover to cover in the Internet age. Readers also find it important to accommodate their own learning styles. This book has been written with a view to accommodating these trends. You can start at whichever of the following points seems most appropriate:

- Start with Part I if you like to immerse yourself in theory. This section offers an introduction to Logosynthesis' history and philosophy. You'll also find my basic assumptions and information on Logosynthesis' roots in other schools of guided change.

- Start with Part II if you're more interested in the method than deep analysis of its underlying concepts. This section gives a detailed account of how to apply Logosynthesis with clients.

- Do you want to see applications in action? Part III contains transcripts of real meetings with clients – complemented with theoretical and methodological comments.

- Part IV describes how Logosynthesis can be integrated into your everyday life, both personally and professionally. You'll also find information on professional development for Logosynthesis practitioners as well as testimonials from prior training programme participants.

Guided change professionals who work with Logosynthesis are often astonished by the model's unprecedented simplicity and elegance. This book provides an excellent introduction to Logosynthesis in a guided change context, but its greatest limitation lies in its nature: the content is provided on paper or a screen. You can't see and hear me as I apply Logosynthesis, so you can only gain an indirect insight into the care, speed, and accuracy of the work that I do with my clients. Many aspects of Logosynthesis' professional application can only be conveyed in live presentations, so I strongly recommend participation in a training programme that's certified by the Logosynthesis International Association.

Please note that masculine pronouns are used throughout the book. This decision has been made in the interests of readability and should not imply gender bias within the content.

I'd briefly like to thank the people who have supported me in the development and dissemination of Logosynthesis and the writing of this book. To mention a few by name: Edwin Meier for the translation; Nancy Porter-Steele and Curtis Steele for their generous donation that made the translation possible; Diana Wesley for the cover; Stacey Grainger for the layout; Ashley Werner, without whom the book would have been published much later (if ever!); Karin de Smit; Andrea Fredi; Nancy Geerts; Rudolf Karlen; Yvonne Mich; Trish North; Richard Scherrer; Corinne Sutter-Meier; Sigrid Stilp; Ulrike Scheuermann; and all the members of the Facebook groups *Logosynthesis*, *Logosynthèse*, *Logosynthese* and *Logosintesi*.

Maienfeld, Switzerland, Summer 2014.

Willem Lammers

PART I

THE MODEL: WHAT IS LOGOSYNTHESIS?

Planting words, which as the trees
strike their roots into the Earth,
send new shoots into the sky,
and give the world the air to breathe.

--YVONNE MICH

Introduction

This section provides a broad introduction to Logosynthesis' history and basic principles. The model is based on a holistic understanding of human beings and makes four basic assumptions:

1 *The lack of awareness of our true nature and task in this world leads to suffering*

2 *The awareness of our true nature is reduced or hindered by introjection and dissociation*

3 *Split-off parts and introjects are frozen energy structures in multi-dimensional space – and not just abstract concepts*

4 *The power of the word makes possible the dissolution of frozen structures and frees our life energy for the task of our existence.*

I used these assumptions and my background in other schools of guided change to create a model that helps people both in their everyday problems and their personal and spiritual developments. Logosynthesis integrates elements from many approaches to self-coaching and guided change, ultimately making a stronger and more comprehensive whole.

1 The consequences of a fall

Lenore beside her shoes

I experienced a turning point in my understanding of coaching and psychotherapy on 11 January 2005. It was on this day that everything changed. Denise, a friend and fellow psychotherapist, asked me to meet with her and one of her clients. She was struggling to make progress with the client's treatment and wanted my input. This client was Leonore, whose story is mentioned in the preface to this book. I met up with Denise a few days before the meeting to catch up on the case.

Leonore's problems had started with a strange trauma five years ago. She was on the way to work early one morning and had fallen on some stairs in a train station. She lost consciousness for several minutes and woke up injured. Her clothes were torn and she was in an unfamiliar place. She couldn't remember anything of what had happened. Her husband picked her up and took her home, but Leonore's life wasn't the same. She could no longer cope with everyday events and was overwhelmed by fright and insecurity. Her fears eventually affected her working life; she couldn't concentrate and was forced to quit her job.

Many doctors examined Leonore and were unable to find any neurological injuries. The health and disability insurance companies refused to connect her problems to the incident at the train station, and she was eventually diagnosed with a personality disorder. She and her husband were convinced that the issues had started with the fall. It was at this point that they turned to Denise.

Denise soon recognised that Leonore was suffering from post-traumatic stress disorder. The treatment process began, and Leonore was grateful to work with someone who finally took her seriously. Her symptoms didn't change very much, however, and she still couldn't remember what had happened on the morning of the fall. Denise eventually suggested that I attend one of their sessions. She knew about my experience with NLP, EMDR, and energy psychology – all models that can achieve surprising results on difficult cases.

The three of us met in Denise's office a week later. I asked Leonore how she was feeling and she immediately told me about a problem that she had had in her bathroom that morning. She had showered as normal but had then become stuck because she couldn't open the shower door. She had reached out several times but couldn't stop her hand from pushing too far to the left or right. This wasn't the first time that she had had a similar experience. She told me how she would sometimes sit outside her house for hours because she couldn't open her front door. She would press the key around the lock but never be able to find the keyhole.

I felt helpless as I listened to Leonore. She looked at me weakly and asked if I agreed with the other doctors who thought she was crazy. My mind raced with neurological hypotheses but I couldn't offer any firm explanations. I could see why she had been diagnosed with a personality disorder; her problems were complex, and experts often use labels to give the impression that they know what they're talking about. I decided to take a few moments to think.

Several minutes passed before Leonore broke the silence. She sighed loudly and said: "It's like I'm living beside my shoes." This Swiss German expression means; 'I'm crazy.' As I looked up from my notepad, I noticed a thin, mist-like shadow surrounding Leonore. I'd normally explain a sight like this as my being tired or daydreaming, but Leonore's words were still ringing in my ears. Could she be 'living beside her shoes' literally rather than metaphorically? Could the fall have moved some of her life energy to a different location? I didn't have a clinical diagnosis and this explanation seemed to fit so well. Leonore couldn't open her shower door or unlock her front door because her hands were moving with her displaced energy and not her physical body. Reconnecting the body with the displaced energy could solve her co-ordination issues – and possibly her emotional issues as well.

The first intervention

I told Leonore about my idea and suggested she try to move her 'shadow body' back into her physical body. She was curious at first, but within seconds her curiosity had transformed into violent fear. This response confirmed that I'd stumbled on something important. I worked with Denise to reassure Leonore that she could stop the experiment at any time. She finally agreed to another attempt and began to imagine her two bodies coming together.

The results were dramatic. Tears soon started to run down Leonore's cheeks and she gasped and cried loudly. I was worried and offered to stop the process, but she was determined to continue. Fifteen minutes passed before she finally calmed down. When she was able to talk again, she could at last remember what had happened on that fateful morning six years ago. She told us how she had been thrown down the stairs by a hurried passer-by and knocked unconscious. She had lain on the ground for several minutes, wounded and frozen with fright. She had eventually walked back to her car but hadn't been able to open its doors. She had then tried to take the train but had faced the same problem. In the end she had asked some strangers to call her husband who eventually came and drove her home.

Leonore looked at Denise and me as if she were going to burst with joy. She was so relieved that we had made some progress. The experiment had dissolved the split between her physical body and her consciousness, and Leonore was no longer 'living beside her shoes.'

The angry consultant

I met with Leonore again a few weeks later. I'd been looking for simple, effective ways of relieving pain and suffering since the start of my training, and our last session had made a strong impression on me. I wanted to know more.

Leonore hadn't been in my office for long when she told me about her latest issue. She had had a bad experience at a hospital several months ago and she was now worried about her next appointment. The consultant who last examined her had suddenly become very angry halfway through his checks. Her new appointment was with another doctor, but she couldn't stop worrying that this doctor would become angry as well.

I asked Leonore to describe exactly what had happened during her last appointment. She told me the story and recalled how the consultant had yelled straight into her right ear. She constantly moved her head to the left as she talked – as if she were trying to escape someone who was standing to her right. She soon began to panic. Activating this memory caused her to react as if the consultant were actually in my office.

I drew on my experience with NLP and asked Leonore if she could move her image of the consultant in the space around her. She replied that she could, and I then asked her to remove the image from this space. Her fear of the upcoming examination disappeared in an instant.

Leonore phoned me a week later. She had been to the appointment and everything had gone smoothly.

A new model?

Both of my sessions with Leonore caused me to reassess my work in guided change. The first session showed me that people could experience their minds and bodies as being in different places. This wasn't a new idea; similar separations are mentioned in all major spiritual traditions and are common in reports of severely traumatised people and those who have had near-death experiences. Neuro-scientific measurements reveal specific changes in the activity of the brain's right temporal lobe that correspond to the perception of such separation[2], and modern physics research is even producing evidence that the phenomenon could really, physically exist. [3][4][5] But what struck me was how the idea wasn't being used for the purposes of healing and development.

[2] Persinger, M. (2001). The neuropsychiatry of paranormal experiences. Neuropsychiatric Practice and Opinion 13 (4): pp. 521–522.

[3] Sheldrake, R. (2003). The Sense of Being Stared At. London: Random House UK Ltd.

[4] Radin, D. (2006). Entangled Minds. New York. Paraview Pocket Books.

[5] van Lommel, P. (2011) Consciousness Beyond Life: The Science of the Near-Death Experience. HarperOne; Reprint edition.

The second session revealed that threatening virtual representations could exist in people's personal spaces. These representations seemed real for the people affected and could trigger physical and emotional stress reactions – but it was possible to change the representations and so watch the affected people react in different ways.

I now needed to develop these discoveries into a system for use with other clients. The system would reconnect people's minds and bodies and free them from any disturbing images that surrounded them. I began to watch my clients more closely when they talked about their problems. I paid attention to where they looked while they spoke, what their bodies showed when they talked about other people who had made them happy or caused them problems, and where they seemed to place their options in space when they talked about decisions.

Alexei's anxiety confirms my discovery

I gave a coaching seminar in Moscow a few months after my sessions with Leonore. During one my demonstrations, Alexei, a 40 year-old psychiatrist, told me about a time when his boss had put him under pressure. Alexei's body twisted into an odd angle as he spoke. I asked what was happening and he described a sharp pain in the middle of his right-hand side. He compared the feeling to having a large, sharp stone pressed into him in that position.

I invited Alexei to visualise removing the stone from his side and personal space. His fear of his boss disappeared as soon as he followed my instructions – much to the astonishment of everyone present.

The power of words

My experience in Moscow confirmed how virtual representations can affect well-being. I began to use this information with my clients, encouraging them to search for disturbing images in their personal spaces and use visualisation techniques to remove these images. Many of my clients benefited from the work, but some would attribute far too much power to the images. The images would then be too strong to dissolve with visualisation.

The power of words offered the answer. I was already familiar with Immunics, an approach that uses specific sentences to treat physical symptoms and chronic diseases. The Immunics sentences dissolve the rigid structures associated with these problems and free up people's life energy for their real missions. I wanted to use this power to offer my clients an effective alternative to visualisation.

I began to develop my own sentences based on energy psychology. I tried many options over several years before I eventually found the three sentences that worked. The first sentence retrieves a person's energy from the distressing images that he perceives in his personal space. The second sentence removes energy from these images that doesn't really belong to the person. The third sentence retrieves all of the person's energy that's bound up in his reactions to the distressing images.

Here's an example of how the sentences could be used on a distressing childhood memory that took place in a classroom:[6]

1 *I retrieve all my energy that's bound up in this image of Mr. Mayer and the taunting children and take it back to the right place in my Self.*

2 *I remove all non-me energy that's associated with this image of Mr. Mayer and the taunting children from all of my cells, from all of my body and from my personal space, and I send it to where it truly belongs.*

3 *I retrieve all my energy that's bound up in all my reactions to the memory of Mr. Mayer and the taunting children and I take it back to the right place in my Self.*

But it wasn't just the exact sentence forms that were important. Equally important was finding the right topics for the sentences. I developed two meta-questions to help identify and simplify the issues to be worked on. These meta-questions are covered in Chapter 11.

---

[6] Lammers, W. & Fredi, A. (2012). Restoring the Flow – a Primer of Logosynthesis. URL: https://www.smashwords.com/books/view/284465. Retrieved 6 May 2014.

Logosynthesis – a comprehensive system

I spent the next few months introducing my clients to my idea and the sentences. It quickly became clear that we're all split into many different parts. We all have personal energy fields around us that are set up like museums, filled with statues of people from our pasts and images of possible futures. We respond to our museums' exhibits as if they were real. The statues and images distort our perceptions of the world in the present, and this distortion has far-reaching consequences.

My sentences finally provided a way for people to reintegrate their split parts and clear out their personal museums. They could now live in the present without having repeated and painful confrontations with their pasts. The power of words made this healing possible.

I eventually chose to call my system 'Logosynthesis.' The name is made up of two ancient Greek words. The first, 'logos', is translated as 'meaning' or 'word.' The second, 'synthesis', is translated as 'putting together.' The combination refers to how words are used to recombine our fragmented parts. Logosynthesis is literally about 'using words to put people back together.'

Chapter 1 in brief:

- Logosynthesis started in 2005 after my sessions with Leonore.
- I discovered that our minds and bodies can be in different places at the same time.
- Images of other people surround us in our personal spaces.
- These images can cause physical, emotional, and mental reactions.
- The images and their corresponding reactions can be neutralised by saying specific sentences.

---

2 My odyssey: Logosynthesis' emergence

ALL MODELS OF GUIDED CHANGE ARE ROOTED IN THEIR DEVE-LOPERS' SOCIETIES AND CULTURES. Just as psychoanalysis has its origins in bourgeois Vienna at end of the 19th century, Logosynthesis is a product of Western society and culture at the start of the 21st century. At the same time, however, Logosynthesis is more. The model uses effective principles from many sources including psychotherapy, humanistic psychology, and ancient knowledge of healing and development. The combined result of these principles is new and unique. Some professionals will find Logosynthesis surprising; others will find it incredible.

This chapter covers two questions that I'm asked time and time again:

– *What models did I work with before Logosynthesis?*
– *What similarities and differences exist between Logosynthesis and other models of counselling, coaching, and psychotherapy?*

My answers to these questions will help you to transition your knowledge of proven, existing models into knowledge of Logosynthesis. You'll also gain a fuller appreciation of Logosynthesis' great potential and insight into how you can apply the model in your professional practice.

Guided change

I worked with many different change models before I discovered Logosynthesis. My initial studies exposed me to humanistic psychology, client-centred psychotherapy, encounter groups, gestalt therapy, and transactional analysis. I then spent several years working at an alpine clinic where I explored bio-energetics and hypnotherapy.

I eventually specialised in transactional analysis and neuro-linguistic programming (NLP). Transactional analysis showed me how to talk to people, understand them in the context of their pasts, provide a safe environment in which to identify key issues, and help to activate their resources. My NLP training taught me to watch people closely, look for patterns in how they process information, and then attempt to change these patterns.

Transactional analysis and NLP are effective models that still help me to assist my clients in many ways. But I soon realised their limitations. Hardly any problem that I treated with these models disappeared completely; suffering always remained. I continued my search for a better solution.

Energy psychology

I worked extensively with post-traumatic stress disorders (PTSD) throughout the nineties. Many new methods emerged during this period including EFT (Emotional Freedom Techniques), TFT (Thought Field Therapy)[7], TAT (Tapas' Acupressure Technique)[8], EMDR (Eye Movement Desensitisation and Reprocessing)[9], and a variety of other models that are now known under the collective term 'energy psychology'.[10] [11] Energy psychology is developing rapidly and initial research reveals its startling levels of effectiveness with mental disorders.[12]

[7]Callahan, R. (1955). Five Minute Phobia Cure: Dr. Callahan's Treatment for Fears, Phobias and Self-Sabotage. Enterprise Publishing, Inc.

[8]URL: http://en.wikipedia.org/wiki/Tapas_Acupressure_Technique, 9 December 2012.

[9]Shapiro, F. (2001). Eye Movement Desensitization and Reprocessing (EMDR): Basic Principles, Protocols, and Procedures. The Guilford Press.

[10]E.g. Gallo, F.(2004). Energy Psychology (Innovations in Psychology). CRC Press.

[11]Diepold J., Jr., V. Britt, S. W. W. Bender(2004). Evolving Thought Field Therapy: The Clinician's Handbook of Diagnosis, Treatment, and Theory. New York: Norton Press.

[12]Feinstein, D. (2012, August 20). Acupoint Stimulation in Treating Psychological Disorders: Evidence of Efficacy. Review of General Psychology. Advance online publication. doi:10.1037/a0028602.

Energy psychology's methods finally made it possible to permanently erase painful traces of the past. My scientific training had previously been limited to biology and psychology, but I was now faced with new assumptions about how people feel, think, and behave. These assumptions included the ideas that:

- A system of subtle energy exists in and around the human body.
- This system has been recognised for thousands of years in healing models such as acupuncture and ayurveda.
- A person's energy can flow or be hindered or blocked in the system.
- The system may be out of balance as a whole.
- Our physical, emotional, mental, and spiritual wellbeing is directly linked to the quality of the energy flow.
- We're able to influence the energy system.

My encounter with energy psychology was love at first sight. I researched the (then new) Internet, ordered videotapes, and flew to the U.S. many times to learn more. I experimented and practised in my professional work, developed my own forms, and gave seminars in the UK and Switzerland. In 2001 I organised Europe's first energy psychology conference and wrote about the model in my first book, *The Energy Odyssey*.[13]

Logosynthesis and other models

My experience with other models was invaluable when I started to develop Logosynthesis. I wanted this new method to cover the horizontal and vertical dimensions, i.e. both material and spiritual concerns. Many teachers have tried to assign a place to both dimensions throughout history, from Plato to Christ and from Eckhart Tolle[14] to Ali Hameed Almaas.[15]

---

[13]Lammers, W. & Kircher, B. (2001). The Energy Odyssey. New Directions in Energy Psychology. Maienfeld: ias.

[14]Tolle, E. (2004). The Power of Now: A Guide to Spiritual Enlightenment. New World Library.

[15]Almaas, A.H. (1998). Essence with the Elixir of Enlightenment. The Diamond Approach to Inner Realisation. York Beach, Maine: Samuel Weiser, Inc.

The horizontal dimension refers to the fulfilment of physical and mental needs when a person deals with events in his material world. Biological, psychological, and energy aspects are covered in Logosynthesis, and all of these aspects draw on knowledge from other models:

- Biological aspects are covered from a neuroscience perspective. We encounter similar coping and processing steps to those used in trauma research. This aspect is covered in detail in Chapter 19.

- Psychological aspects are based on humanistic psychology, and especially on transactional analysis and NLP. Logosynthesis also contains elements of psychoanalysis, self-psychology, object relations theory, hypnotherapy, autogenic training, and EMDR.

- Energy aspects are derived from energy psychology. A corresponding energy model for Logosynthesis is presented in Chapter 6.

The vertical dimension is more particular to Logosynthesis. The newer models that I encountered went deeper than previous models, but the human was still not seen as much more than a biological machine with a wet computer between its ears. Spiritual concerns were consistently ignored. I've always been convinced that we're more than biological organisms. Every human being is embedded in a larger whole that I call 'Essence.' There have been many names for this larger whole throughout history, including the soul, the higher Self, and the *élan vital*. Franz Kafka called it 'the indestructible,' as unlike earthly things, Essence can't ever die or be broken.

Logosynthesis acknowledges Essence and gives it a central role; the vertical dimension is included alongside horizontal aspects. Awareness of Essence or a higher Self provides insight into our deepest motivations. Logosynthesis alleviates suffering and promotes growth, encouraging its users to live lives of their own Essence. People's energy is freed so that they can fulfil their tasks in this world. The power of words differentiates Logosynthesis from other models and makes these effects possible.

Chapter 2 in brief:

- I worked with many models of guided change before I developed Logosynthesis.

- Most models cover only the horizontal dimension; Logosynthesis covers the vertical dimension as well.

- The horizontal dimension is rooted in various schools of psychology and psychotherapy such as depth psychology, hypnotherapy, and humanistic psychology – including transactional analysis, NLP, and energy psychology.

- The vertical, spiritual dimension addresses a person's task or mission on Earth in the context of a larger universe, i.e. the meaning of the person's life.

3 | What we are: survival, competence, Essence

You've gotta dance like there's nobody watching,
Love like you'll never be hurt,
Sing like there's nobody listening,
And live like it's heaven on Earth.

-- WILLIAM PURKEY[16]

PSYCHOTHERAPY, COACHING, SUPERVISION, COUNSELLING, AND OTHER FORMS OF GUIDED CHANGE ARE MOST EFFECTIVE IF THEY ADDRESS BOTH THE HORIZONTAL AND VERTICAL DIMENSIONS. Logosynthesis works on three levels:

1 Survival focuses on basic existence in the life system of the Earth

2 Competence focuses on skills for making our lives more active in nature, in relationships, at work, and in society

3 Essence adds a larger notion of overriding importance.

---

[16]URL: http://www.goodreads.com/author/quotes/1744830.William_W_Purkey. Retrieved 26 March 2014. The attribution of this quote is disputed.

These aspects of our existence correspond with our body, mind, and spirit. They're interdependent and inseparable. Their distinction can be used to examine our lives more accurately, especially when a particular area in our lives leads to problems.

Survival

Biology sees humans as survival machines – 'blind robots that are programmed to preserve selfish molecules known as genes.'[17] Rudolf Virchow outlined this perspective in a famous speech to the Berlin Medical Association on 3 April 1845:

Medical science has recently defined its approach as mechanical, the goal being to realise a physics of organisms. Medicine has proved that life is merely an expression of a sum of phenomena, with every single phenomenon based on known physical laws.[18]

Virchow's view of human beings was purely scientific. This materialist, reductionist, and deterministic approach has dominated conventional medicine since the nineteenth century. The approach has allowed us to study the body's functions in a deep and rigorous way. We've also been able to gain extensive knowledge of the physical universe and its laws.[19] Every one of us still benefits from what we've learnt from this approach whenever we visit a doctor.

The problem with the approach is that it reduces our entire earthly existences to the functions of biological survival. Suffering becomes seen as physical phenomenon, with abnormal bodily changes being explained as organ faults, cell disturbances, or molecular imbalances. Medicine has found many ways to support and repair our biological hardware and delay death for as long as possible, but in the end we all still die. The approach provides no meaning for our existence above individual and species survival.

[17]Dawkins, R. (2006). The Selfish Gene. Oxford: Oxford University Press, p. 237.
[18]URL: http://www.naturheilkundelexikon.de, Retrieved 12 March 2012.
[19]Gleick, J. (2012). The Information: A History, A Theory, A Flood. Vintage.

Competence

Humans are more than biological robots that search for food, avoid danger, and procreate. We instead have a mind, a psyche, that's geared towards processing information from our senses. The mind has its own needs, including for stability, variation, recognition, love, and affection. More sophisticated forms of these needs include requiring a house, job, education, money, and status.

We're also able to set our minds to a communal purpose, e.g. to hunt a mammoth and eat it, to sow seeds in the spring and gather a harvest in the autumn, to build a bridge to cross a river, or to design the computer that lets me write this book. This unique capacity is referred to as 'competence.' Our minds are programmed with neurological software that helps us to actively engage with the world around us and fulfil those of our material and immaterial needs that extend beyond direct survival.

We all enter the world with these non-survival needs and we've built a complex society to help satisfy them. This society has developed a wealth of methods and techniques to reach many different goals and has created systems to teach us the associated processes. Families, clubs, schools, and universities teach these culture techniques.[20] The government similarly tries to create stability and create opportunities to develop society as a whole; the legal system tries to create equal conditions for all; doctors, nurses, and hospitals actively support our survival as individuals and as a species; and a well-run economy offers many further opportunities for acquiring and exercising competence.

Each form of competence is acquired by practice, i.e. the conscious repetition of meaningful actions. We also need feedback from our environments so that we can reach our goals at higher levels while developing corresponding patterns of emotion, cognition, and behaviour.

[20]Sloterdijk, P. (2010). Du mußt dein Leben ändern. Suhrkamp Verlag.

Essence

All traditional cultures have offered teachings about the meaning of life on both the collective and individual levels. Primitive peoples had tribal chiefs for the material world and shamans for the spiritual dimension, while in the Middle Ages the Holy Roman Emperor and the Pope took care of these respective fields. Since the Enlightenment, however, traditional ways of assigning meaning have lost their central positions in Western societies. The academic tradition has taken over the roles of religion and philosophy and the search for meaning has become an almost entirely individual task.

Traditional psychotherapeutic schools offer few answers to questions of meaning. Carl Gustav Jung and Roberto Assagioli addressed spiritual matters in the early days of psychoanalysis, but their initial mentor, Sigmund Freud, did not approve.[21] Freud wrote the following words to his friend Princess Marie Bonaparte in 1937: 'One is sick the moment one asks for the meaning and value of life. Neither objectively exist.'[22] I often meet professionals who see their roles as extending beyond adjusting clients to society's requirements, but this view is in clear contrast to mainstream psychotherapy's focus on effectiveness, efficiency, and economy.

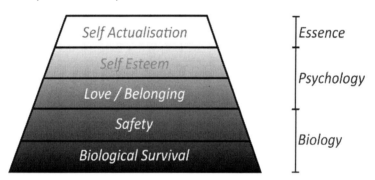

[21]Nguyen, T. (2012). Psychosynthesis. A Way of Openness. In: International Journal of Psychotherapy, Vol 16 (2), 20-28.

[22]Freud, S. (1960). Briefe 1873-1939, Gesammelte Werke, Bd. 16, Frankfurt a.M. p.429.

[23]Maslow, A. (1962). Towards a Psychology of Being. Princeton, NJ.: D. van Nostrand.

Humanistic psychology gives greater acknowledgment to questions of meaning. Abraham Maslow created a pyramid diagram known as the 'Hierarchy of Needs.' Biology exists at the base, psychology is on the next level, and our highest need, Essence, is at the peak.[23]

- Self actualisation: full development of one's own potential
- Self esteem: appreciation of one's own contributions; self respect; respect from others
- Love/belonging: being part of a group; acceptance by colleagues; family life
- Safety: protection from injuries and attacks
- Biological survival: basic needs such as shelter, food, and heat.

Maslow's pyramid indicates that higher-level needs can't be met while lower-level needs remain unfulfilled. The pyramid's upper-most level, self actualisation, includes the following aspects:

- Life goal and task
- Life plans and design
- Volitions
- Artistic intuition
- Scientific inspiration
- Personal values
- Religious experiences.

This top level is largely ignored by modern professional psychotherapy. The spiritual plane remains in the background and is ridiculed or considered taboo. In Logosynthesis, people are more than biological machines that explore, describe, and influence. People also have a quality that extends beyond time and space: Essence.[24] People manifest this

---

[24]Almaas, A. H. (1998). Essence With the Elixir of Enlightenment: The Diamond Approach to Inner Realization. Weiser Books.

timeless Essence at all times and in all situations; it represents our true natures, independent of any conditioning. We know the meaning of our lives when we're in touch with Essence, in good times and in bad. Awareness of Essence is the secret key to understanding and following our lives' tasks.

The Original Self

We're fully aware of Essence at the start of our lives. Babies recognise their spiritual identity and see the world from a position of omnipotence, invulnerability, and immortality. The awareness of this Original Self is soon lost as they learn the limits of their unfamiliar new environments.

Essence has no direct language for making other people in the Earth Life System understand its potential. Babies meet the world as powerful beings but soon encounter the limits of their bodies, their lack of cognitive information, and their inability to speak. A hungry baby can only cry in the hope that its mother will respond. If the cries are ignored, omnipotence must give way to an experience of limitation. The baby's knowledge of the inviolability of its Essence becomes drowned out and repressed by intense sensory experiences. Awareness of Essence disappears into the background and the experience of the physical world is shaped by the biology of injury and the psychology of feared abandonment.

Loss of awareness of Essence is the primary cause of suffering in the world. Logosynthesis helps people to restore connection to their Essence and in turn provides healing. In the words of Albert Jay Nock:

What lies before us and what lies behind us
are trifles to what lies within us.
And if we do what is in us,
carry that out into the world, miracles happen.[25]

---

[25]URL: http://quoteinvestigator.com/2011/01/11/what-lies-within. Retrieved 3 December 2012.

Essence and the world

A person's Original Self can only handle a certain amount of threatening, confusing, or distressing information. Our parents can try their best to protect us, but life experiences will at some point lead to injury and pain. We lose awareness of Essence whenever we're forced to confront the limits of our bodies and minds. The material world eventually becomes our only world and our love, vitality, and creativity become buried. We feel increasingly abandoned, powerless, and vulnerable, and we start to look for strategies to overcome these feelings.

This chapter has described Logosynthesis' view of the world. The view considers reconnection with Essence to be the primary task of any guided change model. Coaching, supervision, counselling, psychotherapy, and self-coaching should help the energy of the body, mind, and spirit to flow freely. This flow is possible if our underlying physical and mental needs – as set out in Maslow's pyramid – are met.

Four basic assumptions about the nature of suffering and healing form the foundation of Logosynthesis' worldview:

- The lack of awareness of our true nature and task in this world leads to suffering.
- The awareness of our true nature is reduced or hindered by introjection and dissociation.
- Split-off parts and introjects are frozen energy structures in multi-dimensional space – and not just abstract concepts.
- The power of the word makes possible the dissolution of frozen structures and frees our life energy for the task of our existence.

These assumptions are described in the following sections and form the basis of Logosynthesis' application in practice.

Chapter 3 in brief:

- Human existence has three dimensions: biological, psychological, and spiritual.

- The biological dimension focuses on the fulfilment of needs that are essential to the body's survival.

- The psychological dimension covers the processing of information and the development of skills that enable a person to satisfy his emotional and mental needs.

- The spiritual dimension refers to the performance of a task or mission through time and space.

- Logosynthesis brings the three dimensions into tune with one another. Its worldview is based on four core assumptions.

4 The nature of suffering

Basic assumption 1

LOGOSYNTHESIS' FIRST BASIC ASSUMPTION IDENTIFIES THE CAUSE OF SUFFERING IN THIS WORLD:

The lack of awareness of our true nature and task in this world leads to suffering.

Entry into the world

A child's physical weakness and mental immaturity means that he has more needs than an adult. Paediatrician T. Berry Brazelton and child psychiatrist Stanley Greenspan have identified seven needs that are common to all children:[26]

1 **Physical and psychological security**
   Children need to know that they're protected against a variety of threats, from environmental toxins to psychological exploitation.

2 **Stable, nurturing relationships**
   Emotional and intellectual development requires the security of stable, emotionally warm relationships. Children who grow up with missing or broken relationships are likely to have less motivation and limited abilities to rationalise situations.

[26]Brazelton, T. B. & Greenspan, S. I (2001). The Irreducible Needs Of Children: What Every Child Must Have To Grow, Learn, And Flourish. Da Capo Press; Reprint edition.

3 Personalised development

All children are unique and so need to be developed in ways that match their natures. Parents and other responsible adults must also recognise individual children's problems.

4 Appropriate expectations

Parents and other responsible adults need to match their expectations to every child's age and development. Too many/too few expectations can harm a child's development as much as too much/too little sleep.

5 Structure and discipline

Children need to have clear and enforced limits. These limits teach them to channel their aggression and resolve conflicts peacefully.

6 Stable, supportive communities and cultural continuity

Children need a continuity of values provided by their families, other children, and wider society. Their environments must also provide sufficient diversity.

7 A protected future

All of the above requirements need to be met if a child's future is to be secure.

A child's parents are mostly responsible for fulfilling these needs. Parents should protect their children and help them to understand life without limiting their development. If a child plays with a fireplace and burns his fingers, for instance, the mother should comfort him, teach him about fire and heat, and explain how to deal with fire in future. The child could then learn the limits of his body and mind while staying aware of his higher nature. The child's Original Self could continue to grow as a vibrant, true Self that knows both the earthly world and higher dimensions.

Loss of contact with Essence

It may seem easy for parents to help their children stay aware of Essence, but the reality is much more difficult. Parents and other responsible adults have their own needs, desires, and commitments that often run counter to a child's need for support and explanation.

Parents have to make money, run the household, take care of other children, and complete many other tasks. When they've finished all of their daily obligations, they'll often be too tired or impatient to fully meet a child's needs. Children have tremendous potential to overcome these limitations, but at some point the lack of support will become too great. A child's biological and psychological needs will eventually determine his thoughts, emotions, and behaviour, and awareness of Essence will be lost. This loss of awareness of Essence is the primary cause of suffering in the world.

Pain and suffering

We experience pain and suffering when our basic needs are not met. Important differences exist between the two concepts, as David Hawkins confirms:

Pain and suffering are two distinctly different things. It is often believed that they are inseparable, which is not true. It is possible to experience pain but not to suffer. [27]

Physical pain has an alarm function that helps us to avoid danger, although we can also feel pain when danger isn't nearby. Suffering is emotional pain that can be caused by lack of attention, recognition, clarity, or opportunities to grow and develop. It's connected to a strong experience of limitation.

Pain is more bearable if it has meaning at a higher level. e.g. the pain that an athlete experiences on the road to victory, a mother's contractions during childbirth, the efforts of an aid worker in a challenging environment, and parents' struggles to allow their children better futures.

Powerlessness and authority

The loss of awareness of Essence makes a child feel helpless and abandoned. He reacts by turning to authority figures such as parents, doctors, pastors, and teachers. The child believes that these people can offer

[27]Hawkins, D.R. (2005). The Eye of the I: From Which Nothing is Hidden. Veritas Publishing.

stability and remove his physical and mental suffering. The authority figures control the child's destiny and win power and influence over his Self. Over time the child becomes dependent on these figures to satisfy his needs. He ultimately loses conscious access to the knowledge and creative intention of his true Self – that which is indestructible within us.

Chapter 4 in brief:

- Children can only develop correctly if their physical and psychological needs are met.

- A child's needs will often not be met or only be met in part. A child's awareness will shift to focus on the fulfilment of these needs.

- A child's awareness of Essence then becomes lost. He loses all understanding of his life's meaning and mission.

5 Dissociation: a key concept

Basic assumption 2

LOGOSYNTHESIS' SECOND BASIC ASSUMPTION IDENTIFIES TWO WAYS in which we lose awareness of Essence throughout our lives:

The awareness of our true nature is reduced or hindered by introjection and dissociation.

This chapter explains dissociation.

Entering life

All newborn children must learn about the world around them. Like explorers, they need maps to determine their positions and set out their goals. These maps are obtained in part by parents sharing their own memories, fantasies, and beliefs about the world. The maps are also produced from the child's direct experiences of the world. The child needs recognition and support for these experiences if he's to stay in touch with the awareness of his higher nature and his life's work. Parents can help him to realise his life task and follow his original interests. In Donald Winnicott's words: [28]

The good-enough mother meets the omnipotent child and responds to it.

---

[28]Winnicott, D. (1953). Transitional objects and transitional phenomena, International Journal of Psychoanalysis, 34. pp. 89-97.

The child is gradually confronted with the facts of life on this Earth. He's initially dependent on his parents for his survival, he can't move freely using his body, and he doesn't know the world's laws and customs. He must learn to understand the world and find a personal position within it. He must develop an ego – the physical and mental tools that are required to do his job in the world. He also needs a language for his vocation and his goals. When support is available through his parents' wanting the best for him, he can begin to display Essence; his life energy flows.

Another mechanism, dissociation, comes into effect if parents are unable to meet their child's needs. When a child is faced with a situation that he can't understand and no parental support is available, the child's Original Self splits off – or dissociates – some of its energy as a coping mechanism. The split-off energy becomes what the early psychoanalyst Ferenczi termed an 'introject.' [29] Introjects are stored representations of everything that the child's senses experience in the overwhelming situation.

Further energy can be split off from the child's physical, emotional, and cognitive reactions to the overwhelming situation. This energy combines with introjects to form 'frozen worlds.' Frozen worlds keep the child's senses alert for similar situations and provide him with a reference set of physical, emotional, and cognitive reactions that can guide his behaviour in such situations.

Imagine the first time that an abusive father beats his child. The child will be overwhelmed by the situation, so a part of his Original Self's energy will split off (dissociate) and form an introject. The introject will store what the child's senses experience, i.e. the image of the father's angry face and voice and the pain of his hand hitting the child's skin. A frozen world will then combine this introject with the child's reactions, i.e. his shaking and feeling afraid. The frozen world will prevent the child from becoming overwhelmed the next time the father acts in this way; he'll already know what's coming. Unfortunately the frozen world will also cause the child to shake and feel afraid whenever the father shows an angry face or raises his voice, even if

[29]Ferenczi, S. (1916). Introjection and transference. In his Contributions to psychoanalysis (Ernest Jones, Trans.; pp. 30-80). Boston: Richard G. Badger. (Original work published 1909).

the rage isn't aimed at the child. This template will eventually extend to other people who look like the father or raise their voices, leaving the child shaking and afraid in many inappropriate circumstances.

Many adults accumulate so many frozen worlds that these energy structures become activated as responses to almost all situations. Such individuals lose the ability to react authentically, spontaneously, and flexibly. Oscar Wilde noted this fact with typically ruthless honesty:

Most people are other people. Their thoughts are someone else's opinions, their lives a mimicry, their passions a quotation. [30]

Psychotherapy and psychiatric literature generally use the term 'dissociation' in reference to people's reactions to stress. The introjects that activate the stress are usually ignored.

Dissociative processes are of great importance to the application of Logosynthesis. The processes come in various degrees of intensity as is outlined below.

The black hole

The deepest level of dissociation is characterised by excruciating experiences of abandonment, loneliness, disorientation, and paralysis. Some of my clients have referred to this state as the 'black hole.' The metaphor is apt: black holes are places where gravity has increased so much that it dominates all other forces in the universe. Nothing escapes the gravity of a black hole, not even light. The awareness of Essence is totally lost in its vicinity. The black hole is associated with existential anxiety and the fear of dissolution and destruction. This form of dissociation is what the newborn experiences when he's confronted with the limits of his body and mind and his parents are unable to offer a protective environment. The black hole is so unbearable that it's suppressed as soon as it threatens to come to the surface of a person's conscious awareness.

---

[30]Wilde, O. (1905). De Profundis. URL: http://www.gutenberg.org/ebooks/921. Retrieved 10 December 2012.

We're totally separate from our true nature, Essence, in the experience of the black hole. This is the experience of autistic children and psychotics, although they're not the only ones to encounter the experience. Many people are faced with the black hole in times of loss and transition if familiar living conditions break down. They're then left trapped in cages of loneliness, abandonment, and fear.

First order dissociation

First order dissociation is our response to events that overwhelm our frames of reference, mostly at an early stage of development. It's triggered again and again by situations that are similar to those original events, either directly or indirectly. The free energy is diverted from the flowing stream of the Original Self and bound up in representations of the external world (introjects) and our frozen reactions to the external world (frozen worlds). If a father hits his son because the son makes an error, the child creates a fixed perception of his father in that situation. The son feels abandoned and concludes that his father doesn't love him or that he's even unlovable. He gives up hope.

This level of dissociation is strongly connected to the experience of abandonment by the people around us. We're aware that our basic needs for intimacy and belonging are unmet and we feel lonely, separate, and excluded from the social world. We think that something about us is unacceptable, and most of these thoughts relate to our parents, e.g.:

— Our parents didn't want a child – not at all, not yet, or no longer.

— Our parents are disappointed by their child's gender.

— Our parents are unable to cope with their child's emotions, thought, or actions.

— Our parents are unable to satisfy their child's needs.

— Our parents consider their child to be too active or passive, too loud or too soft, or too fast or too slow.

These ideas are contained in implicit or explicit parental messages that children interpret as: 'You are not okay.'

Second order dissociation

Most people find ways of avoiding or suppressing the pain and horror of an original experience of rejection. They develop rigid patterns in their thoughts, feelings, and behaviours as they adapt to their environments. They give up their autonomy in the process; their awareness of Essence. Examples of these rigid patterns include Taibi Kahler's drivers from Transactional Analysis:[31]

— *Be perfect*

— *Be strong*

— *Please myself and others*

— *Hurry up*

— *Try hard.*

Drivers are clever strategies for reducing suffering and achieving a minimal level of satisfaction for physical and psychological needs. These strategies ensure that a person is more or less stable in society and in relationships, although this stability comes at the expense of his autonomy. Creativity, spontaneity, and intimacy are all restricted. People who grow up with drivers also impose high demands on themselves and their offspring, unconsciously transferring these rigid patterns of thought to the next generation.

Other forms of second order dissociation include addiction and habits. Drugs, food, drink, work, gambling, and sports all bring people into a particular state of mind that masks pain and loneliness. The pain that occurs in the absence of an addictive substance or activity is often attributed to withdrawal, but its real cause lies deep within the archives of a person's boundless abandonment: the suffering of first order dissociation.

Further examples of second order dissociation include compulsion, aggression, rebellion, and cynicism. All of these behaviours help people to

---

[31]Kahler, T. (1975). Drivers. The Key tot he Process of Scripts. Transactional Analysis Journal, 5, pp. 280-284.

avoid confrontation with the old pain of abandonment. People can also escape into physical symptoms and become ill; some parents give sick children more attention, so a child may develop or increase his symptoms in a way that wouldn't have occurred had his basic needs been met. The three roles in Steve Karman's drama triangle[32] – Persecutor, Rescuer and Victim – are equally forms of second order dissociation. These exploitative patterns prevent the emergence of awareness of abandonment.

Any form of second order dissociation is an attempt to deal with the pain that occurs when a child's needs are not met through bonding, security, and recognition. The dissociation occurs so as to prevent the unbearable suffering that would follow if first order dissociation were reactivated. Awareness of Essence is absent in both first and second order dissociation.

Third and higher orders of dissociation

Third and subsequent orders of dissociation appear if the strategy of second order dissociation leads to new problems instead of stabilisation:

- A perfectionist no longer controls his arduous driver. He's rude to his partner and colleagues because he speaks to them without considering context. This behaviour started out as a solution but has now become disruptive.

- An addict increases the doses of his abused substance but the increases no longer give him the desired stability. The addiction is also a precursor to even greater abandonment; he's about to lose his relationship and career as a result of his substance abuse.

A person in a state of third order dissociation considers his behaviour to be incomprehensible and regrettable on a conscious level. The emotions associated with this level – loneliness, powerlessness, and hopelessness – are very similar to the emotions encountered in first order dissociation, but the underlying cause of these emotions is often unclear. The person suffers from how he becomes suddenly enraged and perhaps bursts into tears. He

---

[32]Karpman, S. (1968). Fairy tales and script drama analysis. Transactional Analysis Bulletin, 7(26), pp. 39-43.

regrets these actions in hindsight. The chaos of dissociative structures causes more and more energy to be diverted from the Original Self. This energy is then bound up until the person's flow of life energy becomes little more than a trickle.

Case study: Matilda

Matilda is a 50 year-old administrator at an art academy. She was forced to take over her manager's role when he suddenly resigned to devote himself to his artistic ambitions. She was reluctant to take the job as it involved a lot of honour but considerable stress and very little money. She's recently fallen out with another member of the management team who accused her of controlling him. It's at this point that she comes to see me.

I ask Matilda about this recent conflict. She expresses a total lack of understanding but recalls that something similar happened nine years ago. Back then it led her into a breakdown. I ask further questions and find out that Matilda's mother died while Matilda was young – and her father had physically abused her. These experiences provided two reasons for first order dissociation. She later developed a second order dissociation as a pattern of accommodation, working hard to get attention and limit damage in spite of her father's violence. She had agreed to take on the new management job as a result of this accommodation pattern; she had only accepted the post to be loved.

The second order dissociation met its limits as a coping strategy in Matilda's new role. She then moved into third order dissociation that took the form of a workplace conflict. The discrepancy between her unconscious motive for the job – attention – and the job's demands activated her underlying sense of abandonment. She tried to diffuse this sense of abandonment with anger and controlling behaviour. This problem can only be overcome when the first order dissociation – the deepest level of abandonment that she felt as a result of her mother's death and her father's violence – is resolved through Logosynthesis.

Matilda soon decides to give up her new management role. She can earn the extra money elsewhere without incurring the extra stress.

Case study: Nicole

Nicole is a 41 year-old writer who's struggling with insomnia and fatigue. She wakes up every day at four or five in the morning, always anxious that she won't make enough progress on her book. For Nicole, second order dissociation takes the form of non-stop work. Third order dissociation – exhaustion and anxiety – is now taking over as her body refuses to keep up with the pattern. I've worked with Nicole for a long time, so I know that relaxation exercises or structured time management won't solve the issue. I instead ask her about the very worst thing that will happen if she doesn't make her deadlines. The following dialogue results, with 'N' standing for 'Nicole' and 'W' standing for 'Willem':

N: Other people will be mad at me.

W: What's the worst that can happen if the other people are mad?

N: They'll turn away.

W: What's the worst that can happen if other people turn away?

N: I feel bad. There's nothing left of me. I'm cold, tense, and turned inwards.

W: How old do you feel? In years or months.

N: Quite young, perhaps two months old.

W: What's the worst that can happen when you're two months old and other people turn away?

N: No one comes back anymore.

W: What's the worst that can happen then?

N: I'm starving. I disappear.

W: What does this look like?

N: I shrivel away.

Nicole's image of the disappearing baby vanishes after we apply two Logosynthesis cycles. Grief then appears:

W: What makes you sad?

N: The fact that I'm still alone.

Nicole now applies Logosynthesis to her unfulfilled desire for closeness. After one cycle of the sentences she's able to imagine making alone time for herself without suffering. I ask her to return to the idea that other people will turn away from her. She replies: 'The other people can wait.' Suffering is no longer an issue. Faced with everything that she wants to do in her everyday life, she simply remarks: 'There just isn't time for everything.'

Dissociation and guided change models

Understanding the layers of dissociation helps to deepen our understanding of various guided change models:

- Analytical forms of psychotherapy interpret deep, unconscious levels of human experience. This approach views second order dissociation as resistance. Understanding deep psychological dynamics reduces these dynamics' impacts on clients' lives. A viable working relationship also enables a second, healing effect: when a client re-experiences archaic emotions in the presence of the psychotherapist, old pain implodes. This implosion allows the client to develop an entirely new kind of relationship. There's now room for give and take, distance and closeness, and holding and being held. This kind of relationship first grows with the psychotherapist in the consulting room but can ultimately be generalised to other people as well.

- Cognitive behavioural models explore hidden skills and resources as alternatives to limiting patterns. These models solve problems or reduce damages by focusing on a client's resources. Clients are taught new strategies and better ways of coping. Second order dissociation is accepted as unquestioned fact and deeper levels of unconsciousness are not addressed. An expert simply investigates what the client wants to experience instead of panic or helplessness. The questioning then turns to when the client has succeeded in reaching these experiences on other occasions. The experiences are combined with the anchoring of resources that can be accessed during panic reactions. Clients end up learning how to deliberately manage their habitual patterns in non-controllable external situations.

— Coaching addresses the role of a person within the context of an organisation. The problems that are processed have three priorities: the organisation with its mission; the intersection of the organisation's tasks with the person's potential; and the person as an adult with possibilities and limitations. Working with first order dissociation is not primarily a coaching activity, although it can play an important role in the process' background (as seen with Iris in Chapter 26). Coaching is more focused on how clients can limit the negative impacts of second order dissociation patterns.

Dissociation and Logosynthesis

Logosynthesis goes one step further than other guided change models. It tackles the problem at its root, i.e. the underlying disconnection from Essence in the person's life that occurs in the wake of traumatic events. The model directly targets the distressing old structures, neutralises them, and activates Essence in the person's life. Harmful patterns end up changing *by themselves*, and a new, living Self arises from the fragments of the Original Self. This living Self remains in contact with the here-and-now and takes the lead in designing everyday life and fulfilling the person's mission.

The integration of the energy that's bound up in archaic structures begins with the dissolution of frozen sensory perceptions. These frozen sensory perceptions are of events that led to the first order dissociation. The structures also contain fantasies of 'what might have happened', e.g. total abandonment and death. The person's resources surface automatically if these memories and fantasies lose their threatening natures. Energy flows freely and is no longer bound up in rigid structures of thought, feeling, and behaviour.

The frozen sensory perceptions contain energy from the person's own split-off parts but also energy from other people or objects. These foreign frozen energy structures occupy the person's personal space. They're especially prevalent when relationships are intense or confrontations with people or events in the outside world were overwhelming. The second Logosynthesis step involves removing the energy of other people and objects from the client's energy field.

The third step in the Logosynthesis process is to retrieve the client's energy that's bound up in reactions to the frozen sensory perceptions of people and events. This energy then becomes free for the client's mission in the here-and-now.

Chapter 5 in brief:

→ If people, especially children, are seriously overwhelmed and left without support, they split off parts of the energy of their Original Self as a coping mechanism. This action is called 'first order dissociation'. The split-off parts are referred to as 'introjects' and contain representations of people and events from a specific time and place.

→ People can also freeze energy in reactions to threatening, painful, or overwhelming events, along with physical, emotional, and cognitive aspects. These parts are rreferred to as 'frozen worlds'.

→ Introjects and reactions to them (frozen worlds) are entangled. Activation of one leads to activation of the other.

→ Frozen representations of the environment can be so threatening that a person develops mechanisms to suppress his corresponding feelings of abandonment. These mechanisms include addiction and driven behaviour. The development of the mechanisms is called 'second order dissociation'.

→ Second order dissociation can lead a person to experience problems with other people in the present as his behaviour no longer matches actual situations. The emergence of these problems is called 'third order dissociation'.

→ Many guided change models tend to ignore frozen representations and reactions that are related to early traumatic events. Diagnosis and treatment instead focus on the client's present situation. Logosynthesis takes a different and more comprehensive approach.

---

6 Life in a museum: energy in space

Basic assumption 3

Logosynthesis' third basic assumption describes the energetic nature of dissociative structures:

Split-off parts and introjects are frozen energy structures in multidimensional space – and not just abstract concepts.

Logosynthesis differs from depth psychology and trauma models by considering dissociative structures not as cognitive-emotional contents of consciousness, but rather as *thought forms*, i.e. frozen energy structures in a person's three-dimensional space. These thought forms provide reference and guidance, acting as templates and moulds for emotions, thoughts, and behaviours. The structures block a person's view of the current reality and prevent direct experiences with other people in the here-and-now.

What is energy?

Energy is the ability to affect something. Energy is needed to accelerate a body, heat a substance, create an electric current, or emit electromagnetic waves. Plants, animals, and humans need energy to live. Energy can flow freely or be stored, e.g. as food, oil, or in a reservoir in the Alps.

Energy is understood to be convertible. Energy exists as physical energy as described above, but also as matter (in a completely static form), information, and consciousness. These terms are virtually indistinguishable from each other in quantum physics, but we mustn't apply energy terms from physics in our context.[33] We're not working with logical explanations, but rather with metaphors that help us to understand complex processes. This use of metaphors isn't new: Freud used the physics of steam engines to explain mental processes, and cognitive psychology uses many metaphors from information technology.

This book understands energy as the creative force of Essence, the energy of life. Aristotle referred to the concept of *physis*, a force of growth in nature that causes organisms to develop into higher forms, embryos to grow into adults, and healthy people to work towards their ideals. Different cultures have different names for this force: the Egyptians had *Ka*, the Indians have *prana*, and the Chinese have *Qi*. Even the scientific concept of evolution may be a well-disguised form of this force.

This subtle manifestation of energy is coherent and goal-oriented. It works in contrast to the second law of thermodynamics, the law of entropy, by producing something new with a higher level of complexity than existed before. David ohn claims that this manifestation can also affect electromagnetic energy through *active information*. Our bodies act as transmitters and receivers of this active information and we're all connected by it in a quantum field, a zero point field,[34] or a divine matrix.[35]

Many biologists and psychologists are sceptical of the concept of life energy. Freud called the idea of a universal creative force in nature 'a pleasant illusion,' and the Virchow quote from earlier in this book makes the same point:

Medical science (...) has proved that life is merely an expression of a sum of phenomena, every single one of which occurs by known physical laws.

[33]Zellinger, A. (2010). Dance of the Photons. From Einstein to Quantum Teleportation. Macmillan.

[34]McTaggart, L. (2003). The Field. The Quest fort he Secret Force oft he Universe. Harper.

[35]Braden, G. (2007). The Divine Matrix: Bridging Time, Space, Miracles, and Belief. Hay House.

Eric Berne, the founder of transactional analysis, eloquently stayed out of the discussion:

Perhaps physis (life energy) does not exist at all, but in spite of our ability to be definite about this subject, there are so many things which happen as if there were such a force that it is easier to understand human beings if we suppose that physis does exist. [36]

Logosynthesis takes a different approach: it assumes the existence of comprehensive, meaning-giving life energy and makes this energy its basic operational principle.

Logosynthesis considers our life energy to be either flowing or bound up in energy structures. The energy structures are the dissociated parts and introjects that were described in the previous chapter. All of our static perceptions, ideas, feelings, emotions, and thoughts are made of bound up energy and can block or obstruct the flow of our life energy.

The active information in energy structures directly influences our physical, chemical, and electromagnetic bases. Logosynthesis' role is to dissolve dysfunctional energy structures so that our life energy can flow and be available for our life's task.

Energy structures and how other methods dissolve them

Logosynthesis considers life energy structures to be as real as someone's physical body. The structures are simple to locate: if you ask someone to remember a painful event, they'll usually be able to find the disturbing energy structures of the people and other elements involved in the surrounding space. Current events can activate these energy structures and unleash the physical, emotional, and cognitive reactions that are stored within them. This triggering leads to suffering. Dissolving the disturbing energy structures removes the chance of suffering and allows the person to be present in the current reality.

---

[36]Berne, E. (1982). A Layman's Guide to Psychiatry and Psychoanalysis. Simon & Schuster.

Roger Callahan's Thought Field Therapy[37] and Gary Craig's Emotional Freedom Techniques[38] dissolve disturbing energy structures by tapping acupuncture points. The Systemic Constellation work of Bert Hellinger[39] and Matthias Varga von Kibéd[40] takes a different approach by trying to harmonise a person's relationships with the figures who appear in disturbing energy structures. This work dissolves the energy structures by helping people to reframe their relationships with the figures.

The Logosynthesis approach

Logosynthesis doesn't require professionals to analyse the content or meaning of the energy structures that exist in their clients' personal spaces. You may need to listen to a client's story so as to build up your working relationship, but the story isn't necessary for dissolving the disturbing introjects. The method doesn't force clients to understand the images of their pasts or reinterpret key relationships.

Logosynthesis sees the problem as lying in the existence of energy structures and not in their content. The energy of Essence must flow freely, and energy structures in a client's personal space prevent or restrict this flow. Blocked energy prevents a client from developing and from responding appropriately in the here-and-now. Removing dusty exhibits from a client's personal museum makes room for new emotions, new thoughts, and new behaviours. Dissolving frozen worlds immediately frees the client's resources and makes him able to solve any problems that occur.

[37]Callahan, R. (1955). Five Minute Phobia Cure: Dr. Callahan's Treatment for Fears, Phobias and Self-Sabotage. Enterprise Publishing, Inc.

[38]Craig, G. (2011). The EFT Manual. Everyday EFT: Emotional Freedom Techniques Series. Elite Books.

[39]Hellinger, B. (2001). Love's Own Truths: Bonding And Balancing In Close Relationships. Zeig, Tucker & Theisen.

[40]Varga von Kibéd, M. & Sparrer, I. (2005). Ganz im Gegenteil, Tetralemma-Arbeit und andere Grundformen Systemischer Strukturaufstellungen.

Energy from other people and objects

Energy from other people and objects can also exist in someone's personal space. This foreign energy can contain adopted values, beliefs, emotions, and behaviours – especially if the energy originates from our parents or our other primary relationships.

Violence and abuse of all sorts leave traces of the people who commit them, as we see with Iris in Chapter 26 who was abused as a child by her father. The abuse experience was activated in our session and Iris' condition improved as soon as she removed her father's energy from her personal space. The same pattern applies to objects, e.g. a car's bumper in a car accident or a surgeon's knife after an operation. This aspect of Logosynthesis often astounds guided change professionals, and psychotherapists in particular. There are few areas within the method in which results can be observed so clearly. Three simple sentences send energy back to where it belongs with surprising effects.

Case study: Renate

Renate is a 43 year-old physical therapist who suffers from the memory of a childhood tonsil operation. Her mother has told her the story of that operation over and over again. She was four years old at the time and wasn't allowed visitors for three days after the procedure. An 'evil' nurse stopped her from having visitors on the fourth day as well, supposedly out of fear that Renate would cry and cause her wounds to bleed. A family friend who worked at the hospital looked in on the fourth evening and found Renate curled up in bed, whimpering softly and utterly inconsolable.

I ask Renate to rate the scene on a distress scale from 0 to 10 as soon as she finishes telling me the story. She rates it as a 9. I give her the first Logosynthesis sentences, and 20 seconds later she says: 'Nothing happened.' I continue with the second sentence and she suddenly enters a deep trance. Her eyes flicker rapidly behind their lids. After a short while she comes around and says: 'It's gone.' Renate had processed the disturbing experience of the operation many years ago but the trauma had stayed with her mother. It was her mother's frozen energy that she had been carrying around in her personal space.

How Logosynthesis dissolves energy structures

Logosynthesis helps people to clear out the representations that fill their personal museums. Clients dissolve these frozen worlds by retrieving the energy that the worlds contain and bringing it back to the 'right place' within themselves. The energy becomes available as soon as it's retrieved. If we return to Leonore's case from Chapter 1, her fear of the upcoming hospital appointment disappeared as soon as she dissolved the image of the consultant from her personal space.

It's important to remember that frozen worlds rarely come from a single event. They're normally more like Russian dolls. On the surface they'll look like Vladimir Putin, but once you've removed the first layer you'll see Yeltsin, Gorbachev, various Soviet leaders, and finally a small doll of Tsar Nicholas II. Representations of past events are often hidden by representations of subsequent events. The following case studies look at how Logosynthesis dissolves energy structures in a step-by-step manner.

Case study: Otto

Otto is a talented young production engineer who seriously doubts his professional competence. He's particularly nervous about giving presentations to his management team. He spends days preparing the presentations but the worry never goes away. He knows that his products are good, but his tension has nothing to do with his actual achievements.

I talk to Otto about the problem and we discover three events that lie at the root of his fear:

- His mother told him off when he was four years old. He had been playing in the family's garden and his clothes had become dirty. His mother saw the mess and became angry when he came back into the kitchen.

- He tried to learn basic arithmetic with his father during his first year at school. His father had explained the topic in his study but Otto had been unable to understand it. He became very good at mathematics just one year later, but the trauma of the first experience had left its mark.

- He wet himself at school when he was six years old. The teacher made him stand in the corner as a punishment. When he thought back to the event he saw himself standing in the corner while the rest of his class continued to learn.

Otto uses Logosynthesis to neutralise these memories. His problems at work disappear as soon as the split parts are integrated. His increased relaxation helps him to become more creative, and his bosses soon start praising his innovative new product ideas.

Case study: Sander

Sander is a 42 year-old social worker who wants to become a self-employed trainer. He regularly holds successful seminars, but he can't stop feeling that he isn't really capable. Introjects of loud voices often tell him that he's too stupid to ever achieve anything. These voices always disappear as soon as his lectures begin.

I work with Sander to find the source of the voices. We establish that he hears three voices that appear in sequence: a lecturer, a schoolteacher, and his father. I ask him to focus on the final voice. He closes his eyes and sees an image of his father teaching something to a young version of himself. His father soon becomes impatient and slaps him. I ask Sander how much stress this scene causes him on a scale from 0 to 10, and he replies by giving it a 9. This rating drops to a 6 once he applies the Logosynthesis sentences to the scene.

I tell Sander to close his eyes again. He can now see an image of himself as a crying baby, and he soon realises that his father never wanted a son at all. His father had been jealous of him and wanted to keep his mother for himself. I encourage Sander to apply the Logosynthesis sentences to this image of himself as a baby. He completes the first sentence but then stops suddenly. He can now see through his baby-self's eyes and he doesn't understand what's happened. He cries for help and I give him three new sentences to satisfy his need for orientation. The image of himself as a baby disappears as soon as he's said the sentences.

I ask Sander to close his eyes for the next cycle. He sees the image of his father teaching him something once more, but this time he addresses his father directly: "I can't learn with you standing over me!" I ask him how much stress this scene now causes him on a scale from 0 to 10. The number has reduced to 2, and he no longer doubts his ability to hold excellent seminars.

EXERCISE: IMAGE AND REACTION

Many professionals who come into contact with Logosynthesis for the first time have difficulty understanding what's meant by 'energy structures in space.' The following exercise helps to explain the concept. Think of someone you like and explore *how* you think about this person. You'll soon discover a representation of the person in the space around you, either near to your body or even within your body. Ask yourself these questions:

— *Where do you perceive the representation in the space around you or within your body?*

— *How far away is the representation?*

— *How do you know that the representation is there? Can you see the person? Hear them? Feel them?*

Most people can see or hear the representation of the person. Sometimes people also feel a live energy surrounding or touching them.

Now check how you react to the representation:

— *What emotions do you experience when you consider the representation?*

— What happens in your body?

— What thoughts enter your mind?

You'll notice that the idea of a person causes you to have an emotional reaction. This doesn't just happen with representations of people you like. Think of someone you dislike and ask yourself the questions above. You'll perceive the representation of this person in a different location around or within yourself and you'll react to the presence with different emotions.

Logosynthesis understands representations to be energy structures. These structures are linked to certain places in your personal space. Try imagining the two representations from this exercise switching places; you'll feel unpleasant and as if you're disturbing a balance. Every structure seems to have its own place. The structures nevertheless obey simple mechanical laws and so dissolve when we retrieve our own energy and remove foreign energy from them.

EXERCISE: NEUTRALISING PERCEPTIONS AND REACTIONS

This exercise shows how energy structures can be dissolved – or 'neutralised.'

Think of the person you dislike from the previous exercise. Consider the following questions:

→ *Where do you perceive the representation of this person in the space around you or within your body?*

→ *How far away is the representation?*

→ *How do you know that the representation is there? Can you see the person? Hear them? Feel them?*

Now explore your reactions to the representation:

→ *What emotions do you experience when you consider the representation?*

→ *What happens in your body?*

→ *What thoughts enter your mind?*

→ *How much distress does the representation cause you on a scale from 0 to 10?*

Now say the following three sentences in a normal conversational tone. Wait between 30 seconds and two minutes after each sentence to allow it to take effect:

1 *I retrieve all my energy bound up in this image of that person and take it back to the right place in my Self.*

2 *I remove all non-me energy connected with this image of this person from all of my cells, from my body and from my personal space and I send it to where it truly belongs.*

3 *I retrieve all my energy bound up in all my reactions to this image of that person and take it back to the right place in my Self.*

Now think of the person again and explore what's changed since you started the exercise:

→ *Where do you perceive the representation of the person in the space around you or within your body?*

→ *What emotional, physical, and cognitive reactions do you have in relation to the representation?*

→ *How much distress does the representation cause you on a scale from 0 to 10?*

You'll probably discover that the representation has disappeared completely or changed into a form that triggers fewer emotional, physical, and cognitive reactions. The three sentences have worked a minor miracle: disturbing energy structures have been neutralised with the power of words. Working with Logosynthesis gives your clients access to this same power.

Chapter 6 in brief:

→ Energy causes changes in the system of the universe.

→ Logosynthesis assumes the existence of a life force that we call 'Essence'.

→ Essence is a subtle form of energy that contains active information. This active information can act on electromagnetic and chemical processes.

→ Dissociated states and introjects are energy structures in space.

→ The emotional and cognitive content of these structures is irrelevant in Logosynthesis. The content disappears when energy structures are dissolved – or 'neutralised.'

→ Energy structures are neutralised by the power of words.

7 Abracadabra: the power of words

Basic assumption 4

LOGOSYNTHESIS' FOURTH BASIC ASSUMPTION distinguishes the approach from many other models of guided change:

The power of the word makes possible the dissolution of frozen structures and frees our life energy for the task of our existence.

The power of words in Logosynthesis

The power of words to effect change has been recognised throughout history in many fields. Healing spells have attributed a special, creative quality to words for centuries. 'Abracadabra', the magic word known to children across the world, is similar. The original Aramaic form of the word, *avrah ka dabra*, means: 'I create as I speak.'

Religious writings provide many more traditional examples of words' power:

→ In the Old Testament (Genesis 1:3): *And God said: 'Let there be light.' And there was light.*

→ In the New Testament (John 1:1): *In the beginning was the Word, and the Word was with God, and the Word was God.*

→ In the Qur'an (2, 118): *If Allah determines a matter, he only says: 'Let it be', and it is.*

The power of words can also be seen in other contexts. The Japanese scientist Masaru Emoto conducted an experiment in which he wrote words such as 'love,' 'gratitude,' and 'hate' on bowls of water that he then froze.[41] When he examined the ice crystals that formed, the crystals in the 'positive' bowls were beautifully and regularly formed while those in the 'negative' bowls were distorted and irregular. If words can mark water in this way, we must assume that they can also influence our inner states; the adult human body is around 70% water.

Many models of guided change are based in biology and psychology – both disciplines that view language only as a tool for describing reality. Coaching, counselling, and psychotherapy do use words to influence clients, but only indirectly through conditioning, interpretation, trances, anchoring, and reframing of one's own and other worlds.[42 43] Language is an instrument in these approaches. The power of words as described above isn't a part of their bodies of knowledge.

Logosynthesis takes the power of words and applies it directly in the healing process. The Logosynthesis sentences cause dissociated energy structures to dissolve. Your life energy that's bound up in these structures then becomes fully available for your life's mission. The healing process runs very deep and its effects are almost magical. The atmosphere in a room often changes after a successful Logosynthesis application; people fall into a special kind of stunned silence. Anyone who's seen or experienced the sentences working will know that their effect is difficult to follow on a rational level. Concepts such as suggestion, affirmation, and placebo aren't satisfactory explanations of what occurs. All that's clear is the simple and incredible power of words.

[41]Masaru, E. (1998). Messages from Water. Hado Publishing.

[42]Bandler, R. & Grinder, J. (1975). The Structure of Magic I: A Book about Language and Therapy. Science and Behavior Books.

[43]Grinder, J. & Bandler, R. (1996). Patterns of the Hypnotic Techniques of Milton H. Erickson, MD: Volume 1. Metamorphous Press,U.S.

One of my clients wrote the following report after a Logosynthesis session. I'd worked to reduce her fear of a major upcoming operation:

It's now Sunday night. I haven't cried or had any other dramatic feelings since yesterday afternoon. It's fantastic! I sometimes remember that the operation is pending, but I don't react in a dramatic way any more. I feel as if the sentences are still swimming around my body, spreading and establishing their influence. Their work isn't complete but the drama is almost gone. Normality and facts have gained the upper hand.

An overview of the sentences

Logosynthesis uses three sentence forms to free life energy from dissociated energy structures:

1 Sentence 1 retrieves the person's life energy that's bound up in the frozen sensory perceptions and fantasies that trigger his symptoms

2 Sentence 2 removes foreign energy from the person's energy system and personal space

3 Sentence 3 retrieves the person's life energy that's bound up in his reactions to the frozen sensory perceptions and fantasies that exist in his body and personal space.

Saying the three sentences aloud activates the energy of Essence and neutralises the dissociated energy structures that have kept the person in a state of suffering. A fourth sentence can also be used at the end of the procedure. This final sentence helps to align and integrate the person's energy system now that the dissociated energy structures have been dissolved. All four sentences are covered in detail in Part II.

Chapter 7 in brief:

- A creative power of words has been recognised in many forms throughout history.

- Logosynthesis uses the power of words to induce change and development.

- The power of words can neutralise dissociated energy structures and release energy that can then be used for a person's life mission.

8 Applying Logosynthesis in self-coaching and guided change

MANY OF MY CLIENTS WORK WITH LOGOSYNTHESIS IN THE CONTEXT OF GUIDED CHANGE. This means that they address their complex and painful issues in my consulting room, with me present to offer support. Other clients work alone and rely on my book, *Self-Coaching with Logosynthesis*, for assistance.[44] This chapter will help you to identify which of your clients need professional help and which can use Logosynthesis on their own.

Applying the method alone

There were no Logosynthesis experts available to help me when I discovered and developed the model. I had no choice but to practise each of the model's steps by myself until I'd established what worked. It soon became clear that I could apply Logosynthesis alone and it would give powerful, often-unexpected effects. I really understood the method's potential when I visited France and could suddenly express myself well in French. I'd never been good at French at school, but I'd applied Logosynthesis to images of my critical French teachers while I sat on the train to Paris. When I arrived at my station I could start to speak with more ease, finally using the grammar and vocabulary that I'd picked up all those years ago.

44Lammers, W. (2015). Self-Coaching with Logosynthesis (CreateSpace).

It's common for people to struggle with Logosynthesis when they first use it. With practice, however, the sentences flow more easily and self-coaching becomes routine. The more energy the method releases, the easier it becomes to face traumatic experiences and recognise frozen energy structures. I recommend clients read my book on self-coaching for more information on how to apply Logosynthesis alone.

When do people need help?

Some clients will need more support. This need can exist for many reasons, including:

- People want to learn to apply Logosynthesis within a safe environment. An expert can support clients in using the method, either in individual sessions or in groups.

- The client can apply Logosynthesis to everyday issues but needs support to process traumatic experiences. The need for support is especially common when processing childhood traumas. A professional can help the client to activate his issues and then neutralise them. Clients tend to focus on the content of traumatic experiences, so professionals are particularly useful at helping them to instead focus on the Logosynthesis steps.

- The client experiences physical or emotional symptoms that are too distressing to handle alone. Long-term assistance from a trained psychotherapist can help the client to overcome these issues using Logosynthesis' techniques.

Logosynthesis and professional guided change

Logosynthesis' simplicity can be deceptive to some coaching, counselling, and psychotherapy experts who are unfamiliar with the approach. Applying Logosynthesis in a professional context requires as much care and control as is used in other models of guided change. I cover the extensive effort that's needed in all professional Logosynthesis applications in Chapter 10.

Chapter 8 in brief:

— Logosynthesis can be used for self-coaching, guided change, or both.

— Self-coaching is an option if the client can free the energy that's bound up in his issues during the Logosynthesis application.

— Professional assistance is recommended if the client needs help to learn the method, wants to apply it to traumatic experiences, or is overwhelmed by distressing physical or emotional symptoms.

9 Neuroscience: what happens in the brain?

Logosynthesis and brain research

THIS CHAPTER CONSIDERS HOW LOGOSYNTHESIS FITS WITH THE LATEST DEVELOPMENTS IN NEUROSCIENCE. No research has been conducted into how Logosynthesis works in our brains, but neuroscientists have investigated two similar models: Eye Movement Desensitisation and Reprocessing (EMDR) and Emotional Freedom Techniques (EFT). My comments on Logosynthesis are based on this research into EMDR and EFT.

Francine Shapiro discovered and began to develop EMDR in 1987.[45] This model involves a client focusing on a stressful event, a specialist moving his/his finger back and forth before the client's eyes, and processing of the event occurring as the client follows the finger. EFT neutralises traumatic experiences by tapping specific acupuncture points on the body. Independent studies have proven both EMDR and EFT to be effective at treating trauma patients.[46][47]

[45]Shapiro, F. (1995). Eye Movement Desensitization and Reprocessing (EMDR): Basic Principles, Protocols, and Procedures. Guildford Press.

[46]URL: http://psycnet.apa.org/psycinfo/1999-13238-001. Retrieved 8 April 2014.

[47]Feinstein, D. (2008). Energy Psychology: A Review of the Preliminary Evidence. Psychotherapy: Theory, Research, Practice, Training. 45(2), pp. 199-213.

Explaining the first step

EMDR, EFT, and Logosynthesis all involve the same first step: a distressing issue is identified and activated. Research has shown that EMDR and EFT trigger the following (simplified) process in the brain for this first step. I speculate that the same process occurs when Logosynthesis is applied:

— The senses collect information about a person's current reality. This information is passed to the thalamus within the brain.

— The information flows from the thalamus to the limbic system. This system regulates the person's emotions, memory, and sexual arousal.

— The first part of the limbic system is the amygdala. The amygdala identifies threats to the person's survival (e.g. hunger, thirst, danger) and triggers the appropriate reactions.

— The information from the senses is compared to the amygdala's archive of previous threatening experiences. Threats that the person experienced directly are stored in the right amygdala while threats that were identified by other people are stored in the left amygdala.

— A match between the sensory information and a record in the amygdala's archive activates an unconscious memory. Unconscious memories are stored in the implicit memory and are re-experienced when activated.

— The re-experiencing of the unconscious memory causes the person to feel threatened. The person doesn't consciously reflect on or further process the memory.

— The amygdala triggers an alarm in response to the perceived threat. The alarm causes the hormone cortisol to be released.

— Cortisol interrupts the flow of information to the next part of the limbic system, the hippocampus. The hippocampus orders information, and information that can't reach the hippocampus can't be ordered or stored in the explicit memory.

— Unordered information prevents the person from adequately understanding his current reality. He therefore responds with simplified reflex patterns, i.e. fight, flight, or freeze.

Responding to stress

Identifying and activating an issue can sometimes cause extreme stress. The person now knows that something isn't right but can't influence his physical, emotional, or cognitive response. These feelings of stress can be handled in the following way:

- The person's frontal lobe recognises stress now that a troubling issue has been identified and activated.
- The EMDR/EFT/Logosynthesis professional ensures that he has a strong working relationship with the person. The person is encouraged to relax.
- An attempt is made to identify aspects of the distressing memory, fantasy, or belief. Individual aspects are then selected for processing. This step-by-step processing stops the amygdala from becoming overwhelmed, meaning information can still be passed to the hippocampus for ordering.
- The selected aspects are activated on the emotional and physical levels. This activation takes place in the posterior cingulate gyrus, the part of the brain that enables recognition of negative emotions and avoidance of their triggers.

Not all issues will cause extreme stress reactions. It's not necessary to focus on individual aspects of an unconscious memory if that memory doesn't cause the amygdala to become overwhelmed.

How the next step works

The next step is to use eye movements, tap acupuncture points, or say the Logosynthesis sentences. I understand this step to work in the brain as follows:

- The record in the amygdala's archive that triggered the alarm is updated to match the person's current potential. The record may even be deleted.
- The amygdala now triggers a lesser/no alarm when it receives information from the senses that it would have previously judged as threatening.
- Information about similar threats can be forwarded to the brain's higher centres without unconscious memories being activated.
- The brain is back in balance and the person can face challenges in the here-and-now with his full potential.

Chapter 9 in brief:

— Logosynthesis works in the brain in a similar way to non-verbal trauma treatment models such as EMDR and EFT.

— All three models influence the processing of stressful events at the limbic system and midbrain levels.

— Successful application of the models requires identification, activation, and processing phases. Especially stressful unconscious memories may require step-by-step processing.

PART II

THE METHOD: SIMPLE, EFFECTIVE, DIFFERENT

No one knows what almost awe-inspiring
energy and power slumbers, undeveloped,
in this small, wired system that I am.

-- ADA LOVELACE[48]

[48]In: Gleick, J. (2011). The Information: A History, a Theory, a Flood. Knopf Doubleday
Publishing Group.

Introduction

This section describes how Logosynthesis is applied in practice, from the moment a client enters your consulting room to the moment this same client leaves. You'll encounter much that's familiar in these pages; building a supportive working relationship, gathering information about a client's current concerns, and processing personal issues are aspects of all schools of guided change. The details will seem even more familiar if you're experienced with EMDR, EFT, or energy psychology.[49]

You'll also find a lot of new information. I provide in-depth explanations of how to prepare your clients, clarify their issues, help them to apply the Logosynthesis sentences, and integrate the model's results into their everyday lives. Studying these techniques will let you bring the unique power of Logosynthesis into your practice – and experience the thrill of identifying, locating, and neutralising frozen energy structures for the first time.

[49]Gallo, F. (2002). Energy Psychology in Psychotherapy. A Comprehensive Source Book. New York, NY: W.W.Norton.

10 The operating principles of guided change

The core of guided change

LOGOSYNTHESIS HELPS YOU AND YOUR CLIENTS TO COME CLOSER TO YOUR REAL SELF, THE MANIFESTATION OF ESSENCE. Your sense of your mission as a human being becomes your focus and serves as a reference point for everything you do. You'll recognise how many of your thoughts, emotions, and beliefs are nothing more than thought forms that are reactivated over and over again. Logosynthesis' unique power lets you redesign your life in the here-and-now.

The Logosynthesis approach shares many operating principles with other schools of guided change. Logosynthesis' simplicity and elegance can at first be deceptive, but its methods work within a carefully constructed context. There are seven aspects that require expertise if this context is to be formed. Skilled professionals will find it simple to switch from one aspect to another at the right moments. The seven aspects are as follows:

- Building a working relationship
- Gathering information
- Clarifying and defining relevant topics
- Providing information necessary for change
- Focusing and activating the chosen issue
- Processing memories, fantasies, and beliefs
- Closure and integration.

1. Building a working relationship

Coaching, counselling, and psychotherapy are aimed at change. This change inevitably creates insecurities among clients. Security is a basic human need, and insecurity leads to fear and disorientation. It's therefore important for guided change professionals to build and develop supportive working relationships with their clients. A client who trusts a professional is more likely to engage successfully with new methods and techniques that that professional presents.

A working relationship is strongest if a client has known the professional for a long time, has come to rely on the professional, and has confidence in the effectiveness of the professional's methods. The professional's reputation can also help to build an alliance. On an everyday basis, empathy and clear leadership are the best ways of creating a sense of security for a client. Training in Logosynthesis can also help you to process stressful events from your own history, in turn allowing you to focus your entire presence on your client's issues.

Some professionals are challenged by how Logosynthesis makes other methods and models obsolete. They've spent many years learning these methods and models, so it can seem disheartening to simply abandon everything that they've gained. I reassure these professionals by emphasising their skills at building working relationships; they've already mastered the most vital principle among all models of guided change.

2. Gathering information

It's important for clients of all guided change models to be able to provide professionals with information. Logosynthesis is no exception. The focus of this information will vary depending on the school and discipline, but all models have the expert listen to the client describe his world. Many people come to counselling or psychotherapy with a discrepancy between their actual state and their desired state, so the professional needs information about the client's perceived problems, self-image, beliefs, thoughts, emotions, behaviours, environment, and personal history.

The successful gathering of this information requires the professional to read the client's state. A client who's physically or mentally exhausted must recover before Logosynthesis can be used. It's up to the professional to support the client with relaxation exercises and structuring techniques from models such as cognitive behavioural therapy and transactional analysis. Only then can the client provide necessary information, absorb new information, and find and hold his focus even after a session is complete.

3. Clarifying and defining relevant topics

Once you've gathered information from the client, the next step is to filter out what's relevant for change. This ability to evaluate and select information is essential for professionals in guided change. You begin by clarifying with the client which issues are active and in which understanding of the world these issues are anchored. Logosynthesis considers all problems to be relevant if they're based on memories, fantasies, and beliefs about the person and his environment, separate from the here-and-now. Underlying patterns in thought, feeling, and behaviour should be examined alongside the issues that are raised in the session. Part III covers this matter in further detail. You'll also need a good overview of the client's priorities for development and change before you apply Logosynthesis.

4. Providing information necessary for change

All systems and schools of guided change give their clients information on how they understand human beings and change processes. The quantity and type of information that individual clients need will vary. You can use Logosynthesis after providing only basic information if a solid working relationship has been established and the client displays a certain ability to focus and self-reflect. You may give the client an introductory article from the Logosynthesis website or a copy of my book, *Self-Coaching with Logosynthesis*. If a client trusts you, you may even be able to simply tell him to say the individual sentences and then have him notice the effects. Nothing is more convincing than the rapid and complete disappearance of a symptom.

My preferred technique for such situations is to establish a good working relationship and then ask the client: 'Is it okay to experiment?' I then apply the sentences and go on to discuss the model with the client if necessary. It's easier for people to understand Logosynthesis if they've already had first-hand experience with its results.

5. Preparing the chosen issue

Logosynthesis can only work effectively if you complete good preparations before any application is attempted. An important issue is ensuring that your clients don't take on too much at once. A client will only be able to address minor issues when he first works with Logosynthesis. These minor issues allow him to gain experience with the method's effects. You may need to bring your client's emotions to the surface so as to activate especially minor issues. More serious issues require calm, patience, and experience from both you and the client. You'll sometimes have to break down serious issues into numerous small aspects to prevent your client from becoming overwhelmed with disturbing emotions. In extreme cases you'll even have to stop and instead work on an entirely different topic.

A good analogy for this step-by-step preparation is the 'salami principle.' You only eat small slices of salami because eating large chunks can cause you to choke – just like you should only work gradually with Logosynthesis because doing too much at once can be ineffective and overwhelming. This position applies to you as a professional as much as it does to your clients. It's vital that you're aware of your limitations; Logosynthesis is a powerful tool for change and development, but it doesn't make a psychotherapist of a coach or a coach of a layperson. Be prepared to extend your Logosynthesis experience gradually and never put your clients at risk through your inexperience. Another analogy may be useful, this time from the diving world: never take others deeper than you've already gone yourself.

A further point is to always ensure that you're applying Logosynthesis to the right issues. Logosynthesis often connects a client's current experience with previous life events. A client's anxiety may not be related to something that's occurring in that moment, for instance. The anxiety will instead be rooted in a traumatic memory that's just been reactivated. Meta-questions A and B are used to focus and activate topics for Logosynthesis applications. More information on these meta-questions is covered in the next chapter.

6. Processing memories, fantasies, and beliefs

It was long thought that methods of change needed to be verbally and logically coherent to be effective. Several new schools have disproved this notion since the end of the twentieth century. The processing of stressful events and the treatment of disturbing symptoms is in fact possible through a variety of techniques – from moving the eyes (EMDR) to tapping on or holding acupuncture points (EFT, TAT) and connecting positive experiences with negative experiences on the neurological level (NLP). Logosynthesis is about dissolving disturbing energy structures with three sentences that are spoken either by your client or by you on your client's behalf. Energy that was previously bound up in rigid structures then becomes reallocated, promoting integration and focusing of the Self and intensifying contact with Essence.

You should always be cautious when you first help a client to process memories, fantasies, or beliefs with Logosynthesis. Using the method before you've established a solid working relationship can lead the client to resist the processing. The client may then abandon the method in the belief that it can't possibly work. Such resistance is most often encountered among clients who have a strong need for control. These clients require any methods that are used on them to be rational to their understandings. You'll need to determine how much information your clients need for Logosynthesis to work. What's most important is simply that your clients trust you. Most clients will trust you in the same way as you trust your dentist or car mechanic; you don't need to understand every step of filling a cavity or maintaining a car engine to trust the results that these professionals can provide.

7. Closure and integration

You, as the expert, create a clear transition after each step in the processing of the selected material. This transition shifts the focus from the client's own process to the outside world. The processed issue is then placed within the context of the client's current life. Depending on the available time, the result, and the client's available energy, a deeper aspect of the same subject or new subjects may then be addressed. The session may alternatively be ended. In this part of the change process you can visualise the future, discuss possible options for behaviour in stressful situations, or give homework assignments – depending on your background as a professional.

Chapter 10 in brief:

→ Logosynthesis' basic operating principles are similar to the basic operating principles found in many schools of guided change.

→ Logosynthesis uses its own specific forms for identifying and activating client issues (the meta-questions) and processing disturbing material (the sentences).

→ A strong working relationship is the foundation for clients' learning and development processes.

→ The working relationship arises from dialogue in which information is collected and shared.

→ Topics emerge from this dialogue that are subsequently activated, processed, and integrated.

11 Focusing the theme: the meta-questions

THE FIRST STEPS IN A LOGOSYNTHESIS APPLICATION ARE SIMILAR TO THE FIRST STEPS IN MANY OTHER GUIDED CHANGE MODELS. You begin by examining the client's suffering – physical symptoms, disturbing emotions, and stressful ideas, beliefs, and memories. You develop your relationship with the client and consider the issues that he presents in the wider context of his relationships and work. You then identify a topic and focus on it so as to make it suitable for processing. Logosynthesis has a powerful tool to assist with topic identification and focusing: the two meta-questions.

Meta-question A is: *How do you suffer?*

Meta-question B is: *What makes you suffer?*

The meta-questions are actually groups of questions that give you a detailed understanding of a client's suffering. This information helps you to develop the Logosynthesis sentences. The meta-questions are also used to help clients notice changes that occur as a result of Logosynthesis applications.

Monitoring triggers and reactions

Logosynthesis examines energy structures that cause suffering. These structures are made up of two closely related components, and the meta-questions can be used to track changes in these components:

- The first component is the trigger. The trigger is a stored sensory perception, i.e. a remembered sight, sound, touch, smell, or taste. Encountering this stored sensory perception can reactivate a previous perception of the world or a belief/fantasy about what could happen, should happen, could have happened, or should have happened in the world. The trigger as an energy structure may represent an entire person or situation, or it may be a partial representation such as a voice, a colour, or a shape. It may also take the form of a symbol. A trigger's form makes no difference to the Logosynthesis application. Distressing memories, fantasies, beliefs, and symbols are all simply rigid energy structures that need to be neutralised or dissolved.

- The second component is the distressing reactions to the trigger. These reactions can be physical, emotional, or mental, and are directly activated by the client's perceptions of the real or imagined world as mentioned above.

Neutralising a trigger with the Logosynthesis sentences eliminates the cause of suffering. This in turn eliminates the reaction; there's no reaction when there's nothing left to trigger a reaction. The energy that's bound up in triggers and reactions can instead flow freely.

The meta-questions allow clients to compare their triggers and reactions before and after they say the Logosynthesis sentences. This comparison is important for several reasons:

- The changes that result from a Logosynthesis application can sometimes be subtle. A client who doesn't notice a change can become discouraged, and this discouragement can slow down the work.

- Sometimes the changes will be so significant that the client won't be able to believe how much he previously suffered. Documented proof of the client's prior stress levels can help him to recognise the change and realise that a problem has disappeared. Energy psychology refers to this tendency to underestimate the intensity of prior suffering as the 'apex phenomenon.'[50]

- The Logosynthesis sentences will often silence a client's inner dialogue. This dialogue will have been a constant companion to the client throughout his life, so its silencing may leave him with a sense of emptiness. Using the meta-questions to compare triggers and reactions can help him to understand and accept the new peace.

[50]Callahan, R. (2002). Tapping the Healer Within. McGraw-Hill.

Meta-question A: exploring the suffering

Most people are aware of their suffering but unaware of what triggers this suffering. Meta-question A can help a client to explore the suffering's exact nature:

How do you suffer?

A thorough consideration of meta-question A involves a search for physical symptoms such as pressure, tension, and pain, for emotions such as fear, anger, sadness, and shame, and for disturbing thoughts or limiting beliefs such as: 'I'm lazy,' 'I'm worthless,' and, 'I'm stupid.' Such burdensome physical symptoms, emotions, and thoughts are rigid energy structures that block a person's contact with Essence and obstruct the development of his Self. These blocks rarely disappear when the person tries to consider them on a rational level; they're frozen stress responses that are barely accessible to rational thought.

Answers to meta-question A will emerge during your initial discussion with a client. The suffering that's explained in his first story will be the reason that he's come to see you. Once you've identified which suffering is the focus of your session, use the meta-question to gain further clarification on this suffering:

- *What exactly do you perceive in your body when this topic is active? Pain, tension, cramps, pressure, heat, vibration?*
- *What emotions do you experience? Fear, anger, shame, guilt, sadness, anger, disgust?*
- *What thoughts and beliefs do you have about the topic? About yourself? About others? About the world?*
- *How intense is the level of distress that's associated with the topic – on a scale from 0 (no stress) to 10 (extremely high stress)?*[51]

---

[51] The Subjective Units of Disturbance scale (SUD) was developed by Wolpe, J. (1969), The Practice of Behavior Therapy, New York: Pergamon Press.

- If a limiting belief is part of the client's reaction pattern: *How true is this belief on a scale from 0 (not true) to 10 (completely true)?*[52]

The answers to meta-question A will help you to identify changes in the client's symptoms. Many people suffer from diffuse symptoms that are made up of many layers which are difficult to distinguish from one another. Only an accurate record of a person's suffering will allow you to identify changes after the Logosynthesis sentences have been applied.

Write down the answers to meta-question A and move on to meta-question B as soon as you're complete. The client will be exposed to suffering while he answers meta-question A, and you don't want this exposure to last for any longer than is necessary. This position separates Logosynthesis from some models of guided change: Logosynthesis protects clients from unnecessary stress while focusing on triggers' energy structures at the earliest possible moment.

Meta-question B: exploring the world

Meta-question A tells you which of the client's physical, emotional, and mental structures are contributing to the suffering. This is only half of the story in Logosynthesis. Meta-question B investigates the energy structures that are associated with the client's suffering:

What makes you suffer?

Suffering is a response to triggers, i.e. energy structures in space. The group of questions that are associated with meta-question B are about identifying these triggers:

- *Focus on what you're currently feeling and ask what's causing these feelings*

---

[52]Logosynthesis' focus is on directly addressing and neutralising distressing experiences, working from the assumption that the client's resources will be spontaneously activated when life energy can flow freely. As a result we use the validity of the negative cognition (VoC-) as opposed to Francine Shapiro's validity of the positive cognition (VoC+). A negative cognition loses its relevance when its validity has reduced to zero.

- *What trigger is causing the feelings? Do the feelings remind you of a person, event, situation, place, task, or animal?*
- *Where do you perceive this trigger in the space around you? In front of you? Behind you? To your left? To your right? Above you? Below you? How far is it away?*
- *How do you know that the trigger is there? Do you see it? Feel it? Hear it? Smell it? Taste it?*
- *What would you call this trigger? What label would you give to it?*

Case study: Francis *(from Chapter 24)*

My session with Francis offers an excellent example of how a trigger can be identified from general information that a client provides. An image of nuns suddenly appears to Francis during the course of our conversation. This image directly influences her physical and emotional state. In the following dialogue, 'F' stands for the 'Francis' and 'W' stands for 'Willem':[53]

W: Guilt is often connected with values, rules, and norms that you've been taught. Where do your values, rules, and norms come from?

F: Ten years at boarding school in a Catholic convent *[breathes heavily and pulls a face].*

W: What's happening?

F: *[Laughs in a strained way]* I'm just seeing the nuns. We constantly had to go to confession. Even a single bad thought had to be confessed. That's bad.

W: You see the nuns?

F: Yes.

W: Where are the nuns? Left, right, in front, behind?

[53]See also Chapter 24, p. 189

F: They're standing behind behind me - threateningly.

W: Do you see them? Hear them?

F: I feel them. I sense the anger that they always had towards us. We had to be good children.

The image of the nuns triggered distress for Francis. Further details about this distress were uncovered with meta-question A.

Working with specifics

People tend to reduce many experiences to single patterns of perception and reaction. A client's image of his mother will be composed from thousands of individual moments, for example. Logosynthesis works in the opposite way, exploring perception and reaction patterns and identifying the isolated experiences and events that make up these patterns.

Meta-question B helps clients to focus on single aspects of memories or fantasies, or on their images of people or events at particular moments. It's possible to zoom in from a general image of a client's mother to gaze into the mother's eyes. The client can then use the Logosynthesis sentences to neutralise this specific aspect of the image. An attempt to neutralise the entire image would probably overwhelm the client, so the step-by-step strategy provides results without causing distress. The neutralisation of single aspects also has a general neutralising effect on all of the client's images.

The client's language

Both of the meta-questions ensure that you stay close to your clients' worlds. Your own frame of reference isn't important to Logosynthesis applications – apart from in the context of the four basic assumptions that form the background to all applications but aren't mentioned at this phase of counselling or treatment. Your own thoughts, emotions, metaphors, and interpretations will only distract your client's awareness from his own immediate perceptions, beliefs, and reactions.

The meta-questions explore your clients' experiences using your clients' own words. You'll rarely add anything to or paraphrase their answers or offer explanations or interpretations of what's been said. You should also extend this self-control to non-verbal communication with your clients, matching their voices and gestures and generally avoiding any actions that could unnecessarily activate their frontal lobes.

Many Logosynthesis trainees struggle with the apparently distant attitude that the meta-questions encourage. They'll usually have extensive experience of meeting suffering people and will have learnt a range of tools for helping these people to identify, paraphrase, interpret, and contextualise suffering. The quiet distance is crucial because it helps the client to open the door to the archives that are kept within his amygdala. This is where painful patterns are stored, and any behaviour that engages the cerebral cortex and the frontal lobe closes the door to these archives.

David Groves' 'clean language' principles are useful guidelines to the distance that's needed in Logosynthesis. Groves' principles recommend that professionals avoid metaphors, assumptions, and interpretations whenever they work with clients. Clients can then develop their own language that gives insights into their minds.[54] You simply need to stay curious at all points, just like my favourite TV detective, Lieutenant Columbo. You should listen to the person sitting opposite and have empathy and respect for his situation – safe in the knowledge that the suffering he displays is caused by archaic energy structures that you can help to dissolve. No further explanation or interpretation is required.

The following case study shows how difficult it can be for professionals to stop interpreting. It's easy to fall into this trap. I was myself reluctant to let go of the time and energy that I'd invested in interpretation-based models and methods, and it took me many years to stop interpreting what my clients said. I was only able to let go when I recognised the power of stepping into the background and allowing my clients' words to take the lead.

54E.g. URL: http://www.cleanlanguage.co.uk/articles/articles/177/2/Gallery-Tour/Page2.html. Retrieved 12 April 2014.

Case study: Caroline

Caroline is attending a seminar for Logosynthesis trainees. She perceives the image of an important person from her past during an exercise. She can't say who the person is but she can see the image just a few feet in front of me. I move so that the image and my person can be kept separate, but she still sees the image in front of me. We apply Logosynthesis to the anonymous image in space. Once we finish, Caroline is surprised to find that I seem more 'human' to her.

Classical training would suggest interpreting Caroline's surprising finding as transference. Another seminar participant raises this point with me when the exercise is over: "It would have been interesting to identify the person Caroline saw. Do you think that you represent authoritarian power to her?" I reply: "I don't know who or what I represent. I don't know what the issue was, but I also don't have to know. I realise that I'm seen as an expert at this seminar and people may respond to this position, but this information isn't important in Logosynthesis. It's enough for me to simply recognise that Caroline's life energy was frozen in space in a structure in front of me. This frozen structure distorted her perception, including her perception of me."

Chapter 11 in brief:

→ Meta-questions A and B activate and focus specific aspects of clients' memories, fantasies, and beliefs.

→ Meta-question A is: 'How do you suffer?' This group of questions helps to identify physical, emotional, and mental suffering in the client.

→ Meta-question B is: 'What makes you suffer?' This group of questions helps to identify the triggers of the suffering.

→ The answers to meta-question B provide the content for the Logosynthesis sentences.

---

12 The word works: the sentences

T HIS CHAPTER SHOWS YOU HOW TO USE THE LOGOSYNTHESIS SENTENCES. The sentences that make up the basic Logosynthesis procedure can be understood as three steps:

1 The first step involves the client retrieving energy that's bound up in the trigger of his symptom or condition. The trigger is a frozen perception, fantasy, or belief. The client takes back the energy from the trigger to his Self.

2 The second step involves the client sending back energy from other people or objects that are associated with the frozen perception, fantasy, or belief to where it truly belongs.

3 The third step involves the client retrieving the energy that's bound up in reactions to the frozen perception, fantasy, or belief. The client takes back the energy to the right place in his Self.

Using the Logosynthesis basic procedure requires a strong working relationship with your client. Both sides should be confident that healing is possible. Experience will accelerate the relationship-building process. I rarely use the basic procedure during a first consultation and I'm especially wary if a new client calls and asks for a Logosynthesis session. Logosynthesis can quickly produce incredible results, but it should always be used as part of an on-going process.

Sentence 1: Retrieve your own energy

The first Logosynthesis sentence is:

I retrieve all my energy bound up in X and take it back to the right place in my Self.

X represents an introject – a trigger as identified by meta-question B. The sentences work best if the trigger is identified as a concrete sensory perception, i.e. a picture, sound, physical sensation, smell, or taste. The more precisely the sensory perception can be described, the more accurately the underlying experience will be activated and the more deeply the sentences will work. The introject stays the same across all of the three sentences in a cycle, apart from in a few instances that are covered later in this book.

Form the first sentence from your client's answers to meta-question B and check that he's okay with your version. The example introject that we'll use in this chapter is 'this image of my mother in front of me and to the left':

I retrieve all my energy bound up in (this image of my mother in front of me and to the left) and take it back to the right place in my Self.

You need to be sure of the sentence before you present it to your client, but remember that you can't make a mistake here: a sentence either works or it doesn't. If you work through the entire Sentence 1 process without any results, simply try again with a new version of the sentence.

Now repeat the sentence aloud in sections and ask your client to repeat these sections:

I retrieve all my energy
(Repeated by your client)

bound up in (this image of my mother in front of me and to the left)
(Repeated by your client)

and take it back to the right place in my Self.
(Repeated by your client)

Now initiate the post-sentence working pause by saying something like:

Relax and let the sentence work. Just observe what happens.

You let the client repeat the sentence if emotions or thoughts take over. Such preoccupation often happens with clients who are new to Logosynthesis and don't realise that they don't have to do anything for the words to work. Some clients need considerable time and clear guidance to overcome their belief that they have to solve all of their problems themselves. You can encourage clients to let go of such preoccupations by inviting them to hum a tune or count backwards as the sentences take effect.

Sentence 2: Remove foreign energy

The second Logosynthesis sentence is:

I remove all non-me energy connected to X from all of my cells, from my body and from my personal space, and I send it to where it truly belongs.

This sentence activates the client's true Self, the manifested Essence, to remove energy traces of other people and objects from the client's body and personal space.

The procedure and content of the sentence are similar to what's used for Sentence 1. Begin by saying the sentence aloud in sections and asking your client to repeat these sections:

I remove all non-me energy
(Repeated by your client)

connected to (this image of my mother in front of me and to the left)
(Repeated by your client)

from all of my cells
(Repeated by your client)

from all of my body and from my personal space
(Repeated by your client)

and send it to where it truly belongs.
(Repeated by your client)

Then initiate the post-sentence working pause:

Relax and let the sentence work. Just observe what happens.

Again ask your client to repeat the sentence if preoccupations arise during the pause.

Sentence 3: Retrieve your own energy from reactions

The third Logosynthesis sentence is:

I retrieve all my energy bound up in all my reactions to X and take it back to the right place in my Self.

Begin by saying the sentence in sections and having the client repeat these sections:

I retrieve all my energy
(Repeated by your client)

bound up in all my reactions to
(Repeated by your client)

(this image of my mother in front of me and to the left)
(Repeated by your client)

and take it back to the right place in my Self.
(Repeated by your client)

Then initiate the post-sentence working pause once more:

Relax and let the sentence work. Just observe what happens.

You've now worked through your first basic Logosynthesis procedure. The process will become faster with time, mostly because you won't need to announce the sentences or break them down into sections. Your client will already be familiar with what's coming and be ready to apply each sentence as soon as it's formed.

What to remember in all Logosynthesis applications

There are several points to remember whenever you help clients to apply the basic Logosynthesis procedure. These points will be easier to recognise once you've practised Logosynthesis' steps on several of your own issues:

- Logosynthesis can seem slower than other models of guided change when you introduce it. Professionals must learn not to rush clients or guide them with 'helpful' interpretations. Such interventions can actually delay the process by activating areas in clients' brains that are outside of their limbic systems. All clients will develop at their own paces. You simply need to slow down and allow Logosynthesis to work, much as is required in Eugene Gendlin's Focusing.[55]

- The Logosynthesis sentences have single, standard forms that have been tested across thousands of applications. The sentences mention nothing but the frozen sensory aspects of memories, fantasies, and beliefs. Don't change or extend the sentences for any reason.

- It can be useful to have the standard sentence forms on a sheet of paper in front of you when you start using Logosynthesis in your sessions. You'll then find it easier to adapt your clients' answers to meta-question B to fit the sentences. Continue having the standard forms available until you know the sentences by heart. Working in this way doesn't reduce the power of the words.

- Ensure that your clients repeat the sentences exactly as you give them. In the beginning you can confirm accurate repetitions with phrases such as: 'That's right,' and: 'Yes, that's it.' Don't forget that your clients will be new to the sentences while you've read this book, practised on yourself, and possibly attended seminars. You can say the sentences in sections if your clients initially have trouble remembering them, as Logosynthesis isn't an exercise in memory training. Exact repetition is especially important when your clients are new to the method. I've heard many newcomers misremember the sentences and say versions such as: 'I remove all of the energy from my body'!

- Remind clients to observe the sentences' effects during the working pauses. Ask them to repeat the relevant sentence if you're not confident

[55]Gendlin, E. T. (1982). Focusing. Second edition. New York: Bantam Books.

that the observation is being done correctly. Watch your clients and don't disturb them in the process.

→ It's important for clients to avoid rational and emotional engagement with the addressed problems. They simply need to sit back, relax, and allow the sentences to act. The working pauses usually take between 30 and 90 seconds but can take up to 25 minutes. You can skip the observation reminders as the client becomes experienced with Logosynthesis and learns to trust the process.

→ A working pause ends when you notice a shift in the client's posture, facial expression, or breathing pattern. The client will often make eye or voice contact with you at this point. You can break any silence that follows with an open-ended question such as: 'What's going on?' or: 'What do you notice?'

→ Ask clients to report on the sentences' effects once they've completed the third sentence's working pause. The effects may be physical, emotional, or mental. Clients will often notice the effects as changes in the consulting room's energy. The room will suddenly feel cool and fresh, for instance, or the clock's ticking or the birds outside will sound louder. The room can also seem brighter, and it's not uncommon for the sun to literally come out at these points.

You'll gain confidence with the basic Logosynthesis procedure as you successfully help clients to apply the method. The transcripts that are included in Part III of this book also provide useful, real-life examples of Logosynthesis applications in a professional context.

Chapter 12 in brief:

→ The basic Logosynthesis procedure involves three sentences.

→ The sentences' subjects are derived from your clients' answers to meta-question B.

→ Clients say the sentences according to the prescribed forms.

→ Each sentence is followed by a working pause for observing that sentence's effects.

---

13 Between the lines: the working pause

EACH LOGOSYNTHESIS SENTENCE IS FOLLOWED BY AN IMPORTANT PAUSE. These pauses are home to a series of complex and intensive processes that neutralise activated energy structures. Clients can behave in a variety of ways during the pauses, including:

- Sitting totally still for several minutes
- Rapidly moving their eyes behind their eyelids (as is common in dream research and hypnotherapy)
- Releasing muscle tension
- Showing a wide range of facial expressions
- Recalling previously forgotten memories that are closely associated with the origins of their issues; intense emotions may appear as a result.

Encourage a client to begin a working pause by inviting him to close his eyes and explore what happens. If a client finds it difficult to close his eyes in this situation, help him by not making direct eye contact. Pauses belong entirely to your clients, and your only role is to ensure that they take place unhindered. Watch what happens, and don't respond to any emotions or statements from clients as you may in other schools of guided change.

Dehydration

Intense change processes require the body to have an adequate supply of water. Give your clients water to drink if they suddenly develop a headache, become tired or dizzy, or in any other way feel unwell at any point during a pause. Water – without anything added – will generally help an affected person to recover quickly. It'll also deepen the sentences' effects.

Intense emotions

It's common for intense emotions to appear during pauses. These intense emotions are called 'abreactions' in EMDR and can be handled with three different methods.

The first method – simply waiting – is my favourite. The emotions usually disappear when the words start to work. Waiting isn't easy for many psychotherapists and coaches because many schools of guided change teach that intense emotions should be addressed immediately and directly. It's not unusual to want to intervene, especially when you first start to work with Logosynthesis, but remember that doing so is likely to affect how your clients process traumatic experiences at the amygdala level.

The second method requires the client to repeat the Logosynthesis sentence that he's just said. This method is useful when the client should assert his authority over the associated situation. Begin the process with a friendly but clear: 'Say after me...' Follow this with the relevant sentence. The use of the imperative is important as the amygdala obeys direct commands without the brain's higher centres becoming involved. The command helps the client to feel more secure and reduces the need for empathetic acceptance of archaic emotions.

The third method requires you to say the Logosynthesis sentences on your client's behalf. This method is used when a client's processing of memories leads him to experience a deep and profound sense of abandonment. The method is explained in detail later in this chapter.

The end of a working pause

The following characteristics indicate that a pause is complete:

- The client demonstrates a clear relaxation response, e.g. yawning, stretching, or laughing.
- The client re-establishes contact with you using verbal and/or non-verbal signs, e.g. opening his eyes and looking at you expectantly and/or commenting on what's happened.
- You notice a reaction within yourself. Your own physical and emotional responses mirror those that are experienced by the person in your office, just as in any other form of guided change. These countertransference reactions are important information sources. My inner tension often increases when a client says a says a sentence, and I realise realise that the pause is over when this inner tension decreases.
- You receive an indication from muscle testing (taken from applied kinesiology) or other ideomotor cues that you understand. I place two of my fingers together to form an 'O' shape and instruct my subconscious mind to separate my fingers when the client's pause is over. I've practised this technique so often over the years that I now trust it above client signals; I encourage my clients to repeat their last Logosynthesis sentence if they re-establish contact before my fingers have opened.

A working pause that lasts for fewer than 15 seconds may indicate that your client is not ready to apply Logosynthesis – or that you need to use the salami principle to divide the target issue into smaller, more manageable chunks. In general, however, the end of a pause means that it's time to start with the next Logosynthesis sentence.

Before the next sentence

It's important to check on your client before you go any further. Give him the next Logosynthesis sentence and have him repeat it aloud in sections. It should soon become clear if he's experiencing intense emotions and needs reassurance of your working relationship's strength. If this is the case, ask short, open-ended questions such as:

- *What's going on?*
- *What do you perceive?*

Give the client the opportunity to share experiences if necessary. Listen with interest but remember that your job is simply to offer an open space in which his energy can flow again. Observe from a place of kindness and don't react to, interpret, or explore what's said. Logosynthesis views activated emotions as archaic reaction patterns that should be neutralised and not confirmed, differentiated, or strengthened. Neutralisation only occurs in the amygdala, but reactions, interpretations, and explorations involve clients' cortices and frontal lobes. The most elegant way to prevent a client's thoughts from straying into the higher parts of his brain is to move on quickly to the next Logosynthesis sentence.

Should the sentences be thought or said?

I'm often asked whether clients should think or say the sentences. I prefer clients to say the sentences for several reasons:

- The professional can assess whether the client is using the correct form of each sentence
- Logosynthesis' flow is more easily automated in the client's brain
- The client becomes better prepared to use self-coaching with Logosynthesis later on.

I don't object to clients thinking the sentences once they've applied them on themselves many times – but even individuals who are experienced with self-coaching should say the sentences aloud if they find that a particular sentence set isn't working.

Saying the sentences on a client's behalf

The professional will usually tell the client the sentences and the client will then repeat them. This process emphasises the client's autonomy and the power of Essence. But as has been mentioned before in this chapter, it's also possible for the professional to say the Logosynthesis sentences on the client's behalf. This is a natural choice in certain circumstances, e.g. if the client has a speech disorder that would make repeating the sentences aloud difficult. It should only otherwise occur in situations in which the client experiences a deep and profound sense of abandonment. The person may realise that basic biological and psychological needs weren't met in the past and also won't be met in the future. The professional's saying of the sentences offers the following neurological and psychological advantages in such situations:

- The parts of the client's brain that are responsible for speech are less active – reducing the chances that the brain's higher centres will interfere in the trauma processing work

- The professional offers the client additional security by implicitly sharing the experience of abandonment. The professional's words still result in effective neutralisation.

It's important to say the sentences *on the client's behalf* and not *for the client*. Acting *for* the client implies an imbalance of power. Acting *on the client's behalf* ensures that the client stays autonomous and his Essence remains powerful. All you're doing is briefly taking on his position while you assist with a very difficult matter.

Case study: Ellen

Ellen is 54 and has been referred to me by one of my colleagues. Her son, John, died trying to break up a fight ten months ago, and Ellen is still in a state of panic, grief, and shock. She and her husband received a call at 3am on that terrible night to tell them to come to the hospital. They found John hooked up to tubes and monitors in intensive care, and he passed away hours later. The image of his body in the hospital bed is burnt into Ellen's brain, and she can't bear to think about it for even a second.

My colleague has already introduced Ellen to Logosynthesis but with no results. I conduct the initial interview and then invite her to say the sentences for the image of her son in the hospital bed. Her trauma is too great for her to say the words so I say the sentences on her behalf. She reports a little less panic when I complete the first cycle. I ask her for more details about the memory and she recalls holding John's hand. It had been warm but lifeless. Re-experiencing this memory moves Ellen deeply. I say the three sentences on her behalf once again – this time for her experience of holding John's hand. Her panic decreases further as the cycle comes to an end.

I ask her permission to continue. Ellen is now confronted with an image of John's face. His left eye is blackened and blood trickles from his nose and ears. I ask her to rate the intensity of this image. Suddenly she understands why she hasn't been able to think about the image of John's body in the hospital bed: the image is bound up with her realisation that her son is gone forever. I say the sentences for this realisation and Ellen feels her heart and soul rip apart all over again. I say the sentences for these torn parts and her heart-breaking sadness comes out one last time.

We sit in silence for a while. Eventually Ellen smiles: a happy memory of her son has shown up for the first time since his death. She recognises that the loss can't be undone, but she's no longer haunted by the gruesome and forbidden image from intensive care.

Chapter 13 in brief:

→ Working pauses take many different forms, from clients being completely silent to experiencing intense emotions.

→ The course of a working pause is never predictable.

→ It sometimes makes sense to say the Logosynthesis sentences on a client's behalf.

14 The phoenix from the ashes: the new present

An introduction to the next stage

ALL LOGOSYNTHESIS CYCLES ARE FOLLOWED BY REASSESSMENT AND REORIENTATION. Your role as a professional is especially important at this stage. Your job is to ask open-ended questions about what the client experienced and observed during the cycle and what conclusions he reached as a result. The questions are open-ended so as not to direct the client; it's up to him whether to answer with reference to emotions, physical feelings, or thoughts.

Examples of the correct type of such open-ended questions include:

- *What happened?*
- *What's going on?*
- *What's developing?*
- *What do you notice?*

Examples of the incorrect type include:

- *What are you feeling?*
- *What are you thinking?*
- *Any questions that are too narrow for the client to answer freely.*

It's important to avoid any form of reflection, rationalisation, or emotional engagement at this stage. Reassessment and realignment require you to work from a position of calm detachment.

Reassessment

Once the third working pause is over, the next step is to examine what's changed in the client's answers to meta-questions A and B. For example:

– *What's happened to the image of your father that was in front of you and to the left?*

– *What's changed?*

The client's responses will often bring up new topics that need to be processed with another Logosynthesis cycle. Some new topics may seem very similar to the topics that have just been dealt with, and clients regularly assume that Logosynthesis isn't working when this occurs. A closer look generally reveals that the client's reaction patterns are indeed similar, but that the triggers for these reaction patterns have altered.

Consider a trainer who uses Logosynthesis to overcome stage fright. The original trigger for his stage fright is giving a performance of any kind. The first Logosynthesis cycle helps him to perform in front of small groups without any issues, but he remains afraid of performing in front of larger groups. The stage fright still exists, so he may overlook his progress and assume that Logosynthesis hasn't worked. The first Logosynthesis cycle has actually changed the stage fright's trigger, and additional cycles are likely to help him overcome the fright in a more comprehensive way. It's down to professionals to document exact reaction pattern triggers so that progress is always visible to clients – however small the steps may seem.

Follow up with future pacing if you don't encounter new topics after a third working pause. Ask the client to imagine a future situation that would have caused him a problem if he hadn't completed the last Logosynthesis cycle. The problem may be gone in the fantasy; the client may remain calm and even show amusement at the idea that he would previously have been distressed. The fantasy may equally lead him to experience physical symptoms or emotional distress. Apply another Logosynthesis cycle if this is the case, using the salami principle to digest the distressing structures in a gradual manner.

Coping with the void

New themes will eventually stop emerging. All of the frozen worlds that were associated with a topic are neutralised; the confronting images and distressing arguments have disappeared. You may be able to move on to reorientation at this stage – or your client may be overwhelmed by the sudden emptiness that's now apparent. The blinding, deafening world of introjects has fallen away and the client realises that these familiar energy structures played an important stabilising role in his life. The void is associated with early, wordless, imageless emotional states – the black hole from Chapter 5. A client who experiences this type of disorientation may display all of the standard symptoms of depression.

Supporting clients who face this issue is an important part of working with Logosynthesis. You can help directly by saying the Logosynthesis sentences on the client's behalf. It's also important to encourage the client to rest and relax. Living with distressing frozen worlds inevitably leaves a client's body exhausted, and this exhaustion can reinforce feelings of emptiness. Clients need time to recover after introjects are neutralised. More time will be required if an introject was especially persistent. Clients who are provided with support and time to relax will eventually recognise their inner voices, their callings, in their everyday lives. This recognition ends feelings of emptiness; it becomes clear that the void isn't so empty after all.

Reorientation

Reorientation is about integrating Logosynthesis' results into a client's everyday frame of reference. The stage begins when all current themes have been handled and the client has overcome the fear of the void. A crucial element of reorientation is remembering Logosynthesis' limits, e.g. someone who fails to write a book because of a frozen world doesn't immediately become an author when this frozen world is dissolved. Similar deficits can exist on an emotional level. Logosynthesis showed one of my clients that he always avoided conflict and gave in to what other people wanted. When he neutralised the memories behind these patterns, he realised that he had no meaningful strategies for dealing with interpersonal differences. He needed to take a course in conflict management to gain these skills and give validity to his opinions.

Good counselling is about helping clients to make new starts as much as neutralising distressing energy structures. Some clients will need general coaching, career counselling, or additional training, while others will simply need to learn how to ask for help in realising their goals.

The fourth sentence

You'll eventually complete both reassessment and reorientation. My Italian colleague, Andrea Fredi, developed a final Logosynthesis sentence to use at this point:

I tune all of my systems to this new awareness.

Saying the fourth Logosynthesis sentence normally brings about a deep sense of relaxation. The sentence can't be used until all other aspects of a Logosynthesis process are complete; it should only be said when a client's distress level has sunk to a zero on the distress scale and he feels powerful, alive, and relaxed. It's best seen as the icing on the cake that brings about a further deepening of the client's new state.

Chapter 14 in brief:

— The three Logosynthesis sentences and their pauses often lead to significant changes in perception, feeling, and thought. Stabilising these changes requires reassessment, i.e. comparing the client's previous state with how he now assesses a situation.

— Reassessment highlights the difference between the client's world before and after the Logosynthesis application.

— The next stage is reorientation, which involves matching a client's abilities and position to his new frame of reference.

— Sentence 4 can be said when the client reaches the end of an entire Logosynthesis process: *I tune all of my systems to this new awareness.*

15 Puzzle pieces I: the triggers

Elements of experience as energy structures

I DEVELOPED LOGOSYNTHESIS BASED ON NUMEROUS OBSERVATI-ONS AND ASSUMPTIONS:

→ Previous experiences play major, decisive roles in a person's present

→ Previous experiences exist as energy structures in space

→ These energy structures are made up of many aspects and layers. The aspects and layers can be neutralised with the Logosynthesis sentences.

I relied on these observations and assumptions when I wrote my first book on Logosynthesis in 2008.[56] Back then I applied the Logosynthesis sentences to anything that a client saw, heard, smelt, felt, thought, or believed. I've since made other observations that reveal huge differences between energy structures:

→ Some energy structures represent a person's body, other people, or objects. These structures are now called 'triggers' as they trigger physical, emotional, and cognitive response patterns in a person's present. The image of an uncle causes discomfort if someone was abused, for instance, or the sound of a plane causes panic in someone experienced bombings during a war.

→ Other energy structures represent human reactions to representations of the world. These structures are now called 'reactions' and include physical feelings, emotions, and thoughts.

[56]Lammers, W. (2008). Logosynthesis. Change through the Magic of Words. Maienfeld: ias.

Triggers and reactions are not always easy to differentiate, and the difference between them is a constant discussion topic in professional training. When you come to recognise the difference, your work will become easier for both you and your clients. Meta-questions A and B have been designed to help you with the differentiation task.

This chapter discusses triggers. Triggers are critical in Logosynthesis because no reactions would exist without them. There are many forms of triggers and this chapter won't cover them all – just as the next chapter on reactions won't cover all reaction forms. I believe the most important trigger forms to be:

- Memories (as frozen perceptions)
- Fantasies, hopes, illusions, desires, and wishes
- Beliefs and values
- Physical symptoms.

Memories, fantasies, and beliefs are energy structures in space that act as the building blocks for the world that we experience. All Logosynthesis applications are in some way related to sensory representations of memories, fantasies, or beliefs. Hopes, illusions, desires, and wishes are special forms of fantasy energy structures, and values are special forms of belief energy structures. Physical symptoms are a special case that is covered at this chapter's end.

Memories

It's simple to see that memories can trigger reactions in a person's present. It makes sense that someone who was repeatedly traumatised as a child expects to experience similar traumas as an adult. Events in the present activate memories, and this means that memories are directly connected to a person's perceptions of his physical environment.

A memory can be based on all of the senses or on one or more modalities of perception. NLP uses the following formula to summarise answers to the question: 'What do you perceive?':

$f(VAKOG)$

In words, this formula states that perception is a function of any of the five senses – visual (V), auditory (A), kinaesthetic (K), olfactory (O), and gustatory (G) – at a given moment. The formula can be expanded to cover a remembered event by adding a superscript 'r':

$$f(VAKOG)^r$$

You may sometimes find yourself feeling uncomfortable when you're in a particular situation or around a particular person – even though there doesn't seem to be any reason for your discomfort in that moment. Remember that memories are rooted in perceptions and perceptions are rooted in all of the five senses. Look for memories that may be activated by the person or situation; do you see, hear, feel, taste, or smell anything familiar? Memories are almost always present in your personal space, and these memories act as triggers.

One moment's perception can solidify into an energetic structure in space/time and become a part of your frame of reference. The structure may be more or less meaningful. I recently saw a television programme about a climber who had been involved in a serious mountaineering accident. He had fallen down a mountainside while climbing alone and had been pinned to the ground by a huge rock until another climber found him several days later. He spent those solitary days looking up at the clear blue sky and thinking that he was going to die. The programme saw him return to the scene of the accident. He became overwhelmed as soon as he saw the familiar scenes again; he was internally reliving all of the pain, fear, and hopelessness that had absorbed him throughout his ordeal. He also felt a heavy pressure on his chest – just like the huge rock was pinning him to the ground once more.

Case study: Martha

Martha has been self-employed for a long time but her business is failing. She's in financial trouble and needs to look for a job. She avoids applying time and time again, doubting that she's good enough for any of the positions that interest her. I discuss the situation with her and it soon becomes clear that her biggest fear is rejection. She knows that rejection is a part of all application processes, but this understanding doesn't change the fear and the corresponding avoidance behaviour.

I ask Martha how long she's known the emotions associated with rejection. She remembers a situation at school when she felt rejected by her classmates. She also remembers how her sisters always made fun of her. I encourage her to look further back in time. She recalls an assault that took place when she was four years old. She had approached a man she knew and he had groped her.

I help Martha to apply the Logosynthesis sentences to her memory of the groping incident. When we finish the first sentence, she says that she feels as if she's under water. I encourage her to repeat the first sentence. When she's done this, she says that her thoughts have wandered to her job application letters. After the second sentence she becomes less tense and begins to feel tired. I encourage her to have a drink of water. We then start to work on the third sentence. She soon reports that her lower body feels relaxed but her upper body is holding in rage.

The next Logosynthesis cycle sees Martha focus on an image of her attacker. He's the target of her rage. She falls silent after the second cycle is complete. She can now see the groping incident from the perspective of an outraged adult woman who wants to intervene. The next step is another Logosynthesis cycle to apply the sentences to this new perspective. She still feels indignant after the first sentence of this cycle, but after the second and third sentences she starts to yawn and appear relaxed. When I ask what she now thinks of the job applications, she soberly replies, "It's just a scheduling thing. I'll start work tomorrow afternoon." Her homework is to complete one application a day before our next appointment.

Fantasies, hopes, illusions, and desires

Children live in a magical reality during the early stages of their development. They're unable to distinguish the facts of the adult world from this reality. Many children whose parents are suffering secretly believe themselves to be the cause of this pain. Siblings die and parents separate – and children seek responsibility for these sad occurrences in their own imperfections or perceived wickedness.

The inability to separate truth from reality extends into many people's adult lives. The German novelist Juli Zeh summarised this common problem in one of her books: 'There's life and then there's the stories. The curse of man is to be unable to distinguish between the two.'[57]

When a client comes to you with an issue, one of your first questions will usually be: 'What happened?' Few clients will have trouble with this question, but identifying the issues that lie behind the distressing event can be much more difficult. Useful additional questions include:

- *What could have happened?*
- *What would have happened if…?*
- *What else could happen?*

These questions explore fantasies, hopes, illusions, and desires. These energy structures are very similar to memories, but instead of relating to the perceived past they relate to ideas about how the world is, could be, or should be. They're formed from all of the five senses, so the VAKOG formula can again apply – but now with a superscript 'i' that stands for 'imagined':

$$f(VAKOG)^i$$

Fantasies, hopes, illusions, and desires prevent awareness of what's actually happening in the present. A person's reactions to situations can therefore seem incomprehensible to other people, e.g. someone becoming afraid at even the thought of becoming stuck in a lift. Logosynthesis helps clients to break down the energy structures that trigger these reactions. The work is done in exactly the same way as work on memories:

- Identify the thoughts, concepts, and ideas of the limiting fantasy/hope/ illusion/desire. Some clients will feel you that you're not taking them seriously if you refer to their problem as a fantasy/hope/illusion/desire. You may need to explore their problem with them and explain why you're using these terms.

- Find a representation of the fantasy/hope/illusion/desire in the client's body or personal space. Use meta-question B for assistance and remember the adapted formula: $f(VAKOG)^i$

[57]Zeh, J. (2009). Schilf. BTB Verlag.

- Explore the client's physical, emotional, and cognitive reactions to the fantasy/hope/illusion/desire. Work out his corresponding levels of distress using meta-question A.
- Develop the Logosynthesis sentences for the client's representation of the fantasy/hope/illusion/desire.

It's not uncommon to encounter resistance from clients who struggle to believe that their perceptions are controlled by subconscious fantasies. The following 'ultimate disaster' interview technique can be used to highlight the importance of fantasies. 'Cl' stands for the 'client' and 'W' stands for 'Willem':

Cl: I can't let go of the job.

W: What's the worst that could happen?

Cl: I wouldn't find a new job.

W: What's the worst that could happen then?

Cl: I'd have no money.

W: What's the worst that could happen then?

Cl: I'd lose my home.

W: What's the worst that could happen then?

Cl: My wife would leave me.

W: What's the worst that could happen then?

Cl: I'd be alone.

W: Did you ever feel very alone?

Cl: Yes, when I was three years old and my parents separated.

W: What was the worst thing that could have happened at that time?

Cl: I could have died!

At this point I explored what dying actually looked like with the client. The disaster fantasy was then neutralised with three Logosynthesis sentences. When it came to reassessing the situation, the client discovered that a wealth of options existed for shaping his future with more freedom.

Case study: Fiona

Fiona is a 52 year-old scientist who's very nervous about an upcoming doctor's appointment. The appointment is a follow-up to a recent breast cancer screening. Previous investigations haven't revealed any suspicious growths, but this knowledge isn't reducing her anxiety. Her worst fantasy is dying of cancer and her 14 year-old daughter having to grow up without her. Fiona rates the fear associated with this fantasy as between an 8 and a 9.

I help Fiona through the three Logosynthesis sentences, focusing on the image of her daughter growing up without her. She quickly improves. She feels able to live in the present and can see that her daughter would be strong enough to find her way with her father's support. The fear level drops to a 5 and is now focused on her notion of receiving 'inhumane' treatment in hospital. She goes through another cycle for the 'desire for humane treatment.' The distress now falls to a 3 and she realises that she's mature enough to tell her doctors how she wants to be treated.

Wishes

God, grant me the serenity to accept the things I cannot change, the courage to change the things I can, and the wisdom to know the difference.[58]

Wishes are specific forms of fantasy that exist throughout our lives but rarely reach the surfaces of our conscious minds. Children wish for perfect parents who recognise and fulfil their needs, while adults wish for an ideal partner, a

[58]URL: http://en.wikipedia.org/wiki/Serenity_Prayer. Retrieved 6 May 2014.

good education, a perfect job, a more relaxed boss, a nicer place in which to live, or a better school for their children. The tension that exists between reality and what's wished for often leads to physical and emotional stress.

You can discover a client's wishes by using questions such as the following when the client presents you with a problem:

- *What should have happened?*
- *What could have happened?*
- *What would need to happen?*
- *What should happen now?*
- *What could happen now?*
- *What do you want to happen now?*

The Logosynthesis sentences are applied to wishes in a similar way as to memories. You begin by asking the person to find his wish in its fulfilled form as a representation in space. You then ask the meta-questions and apply the first two sentences. The third sentence is slightly different from normal:

> *I retrieve all my energy bound up in all my reactions to the fact that [this wish] was not fulfilled and cannot be fulfilled, and I take it back to the right place in my Self.*

This updated sentence form reduces tension that exists between the client's desired and actual realities. The client can then adapt the wish to match reality instead of hoping that reality will match the wish. When the process is complete, the client will finally see the world as it actually is – as in the following short poem from Jorge Bucay:

> *Reality is not like I would like to have it.*
> *It is not as it should be.*
> *It is not like they told me it is.*
> *It is not like it once was.*
> *Neither is it like it will be tomorrow.*
> *The reality around me is like it is.*[59]

[59]Bucay, J. (2013). Let Me Tell You a Story: A New Approach to Healing through the Art of Storytelling. Europa Editions.

Case study: Daniela

Daniela is 40 years old and the mother of two children. She's extremely unsettled when she comes to see me. She had to pick her son up from school yesterday because he was suffering from a severe headache and fever. Last night had been torture; the headache wasn't dangerous for her son, but it had triggered powerful memories for Daniela of her sister's death. Her 10 year-old sister had died from a brain tumour when she was only 14. The event had shocked Daniela because she hadn't understood that her sister was so ill. Her parents had also left her alone to deal with her grief, even at the funeral. The whole experience led her to the irrational conclusions that she had no right to receive attention and support and shouldn't be a burden to anyone.

Our first Logosynthesis application focuses on Daniela's belief that: 'I shouldn't be a burden to anyone.' She leaves my office relieved and with a relaxed smile on her face. We've dealt with the stress that was triggered when she unexpectedly had to pick her son up from school, although it's clear that we have more work to do.

The main theme of our second session is her wish that she had had ideal parents. She's carried enormous rage since her sister's death; she's convinced that her parents should have been there for her at that time. This conviction is legitimate and understandable but could never have been fulfilled. Her parents were frozen in their own grief and could neither recognise nor satisfy their daughter's needs.

I encourage Daniela to find her 'ideal parents' in her personal space. We then apply two Logosynthesis cycles to these images. Her ideal parents cease to exist and she suddenly realises how much she's achieved even without parental support. She has fantastic children and is a good mother. Daniela's rage at her parents disappears.

Beliefs

Beliefs and convictions can limit growth, especially when they're negative and interfere with our life mission. These ideas form the framework of our thinking, and our behaviour only changes in a lasting way when we alter them.

I'm always reminded of a university professor I once knew when I think about this topic. The professor stabilised his view of the world with two complementary beliefs: 'I'm stupid' and 'I'm lazy.' If he read an academic article that presented a new idea, he took the article as confirmation that he was stupid. Why hadn't the idea already occurred to him? If the article presented an idea with which he was already familiar, he took this as confirmation that he was lazy. Why hadn't he written the article himself? The man was extremely intelligent but never questioned this self-destructive pattern.

Beliefs and convictions cover several topics:

— Beliefs about one's own identity

People can be unhappy and have a heartfelt desire for a better life, but even the happiest experiences won't create this result if the people believe that they're too short/old/fat etc. to be happy. On the other hand, people who believe themselves to be happy people will remain happy even in difficult and unpleasant situations.

— Beliefs about one's own potential

Students who believe that they'll pass a test have a greater chance of actually passing. The opposite is true for students who believe that they'll fail a test. Beliefs and convictions about one's own potential become self-fulfilling prophecies.

— Beliefs about cause and effect

Many people are quick to connect facts with behaviours and events. If a football player misses a penalty because he isn't wearing his lucky boots, he'll miss the next penalty as well unless he puts the boots on.

— Beliefs about life in general

Images of people, relationships, objects, and characteristics are used to construct frameworks of thought that help to structure, understand, and stabilise life. A woman may be reassured by her belief that everyone has a single soul mate – and she may remain convinced of this idea even as she gets married for the third or fourth time.

Your professional ear is an important tool for helping clients to resolve limiting beliefs. People need beliefs to map reality, and giving up these ideas about the world can lead to insecurity. A good working relationship allows you to overcome this insecurity and question whatever a client says. Limiting beliefs are otherwise treated like all other energy constructs:

- Identify the limiting belief with care, caution, and respect for the client. You'll often need to adopt an almost naïve approach when you attempt to identify core beliefs, e.g. 'If I understand you correctly, you're convinced that…'

- Find a representation of the belief in the client's personal space. Use meta-question B to help with this process. Clients will usually perceive a belief's words as an image or as written on paper or etched in stone. Other clients may hear the belief, often connected to a memory of a person who represented the belief, e.g. the voice of the client's father telling that him that he has to work hard.

- Explore the client's reactions to the belief by using meta-question A. Sometimes a client will 'feel' a belief in his body, e.g. 'I feel that I believe in love at first sight.' You then have to explain that beliefs must originally have been read or heard as opposed to felt. The physical sensation is just a reaction to what's been read or heard.

- Determine the truth of the client's limiting belief on a scale from 0 to 10, where 0 is 'Entirely false' and 10 is 'Entirely true'.

- Give the sentences for the representation of the belief in the client's personal space.

- Now explore the truth of the limiting belief once again. Watch for differences in the ratings and the wording of the belief. It'll usually become more vague or less important – or will simply disappear altogether.

- Begin a new Logosynthesis cycle if earlier introjects emerge for the belief.

Case study: Kyra

Kyra is a 45 year-old teacher who wants to write a book. She keeps putting off the writing because – for unknown reasons – she believes that writing is a lonely activity. We explore this belief more closely and an image surfaces of a stuffy classroom with an ugly, bare desk. I encourage Kyra to retrieve her energy from this image. Another image appears as soon as she's done this. This time the image is of a beautiful table in a splendid house. The table is next to a window that looks out onto a garden in full bloom. Kyra suddenly regrets not bringing her laptop with her to the session; she can't start writing on the train journey home.

Values

A value is a special form of belief that's often shared by many people or an entire society. Values appear in all longer change processes and can trigger particularly intense emotions. It's worthwhile exploring a client's value system and considering whether this system is damaging his development. Damaging systems should be neutralised, e.g. a painter or musician generally shouldn't value precision to the same degree as an aeroplane mechanic or an accountant. Neutralising a value system allows the energy that's stored within it to flow again. The system's purpose then becomes immediately clear and the client can make his own decision about whether to continue living by its rules.

Physical symptoms as triggers

I regularly see clients who want me to make physical symptoms disappear. Logosynthesis doesn't pretend to be able to heal the body. Spectacular results have been documented, but the approach isn't a substitute for medical treatment of any kind. Logosynthesis can nevertheless reduce the suffering that physical symptoms trigger by encouraging clients to perceive their bodies and symptoms in different ways. This altered perception helps clients to change the demands that they place on their bodies, accept chronic illnesses, give up bad habits, or consider new treatment options.

Different people view their bodies in different ways. Perspectives include:

- The body is a complex biochemical and physiological machine that serves my goals as a craftsman, athlete, or soldier. Injuries or weaknesses should be treated chemically or with physical interventions. Men are especially susceptible to this perspective.
- The body is assigned to me by fate. You can struggle against fate or submit to it.
- The body is my window on the world.
- The body is a manifestation of energy that obeys the same physical laws as any other energy form.

Clients' views of their bodies influence the ways in which they manage physical symptoms. Working with memories, fantasies, and beliefs can reduce distress caused by chronic illness. This reduction in emotional burden can in turn have positive effects on healing.

Case study: Brigitte

The following example illustrates how detective work can uncover clients' ideas about a perfect body. Brigitte is worried about an upcoming hip joint replacement operation. The analysis below precedes my use of meta-questions A and B and the application of the Logosynthesis sentences. 'B' stands for the 'Brigitte' and 'W' stands for 'Willem':

W: Why do you have a problem with the new hip joint? Why are you so attached to the old joint that no longer works?

B: I think it's really just the idea.

W: I'm interested in this idea. You're investing energy in the idea of being without the original joint. Why is the idea so unpleasant?

B: [Laughs] It's just knowing that I'm not 100% original.

W: Let's explore this further. What's so dramatic about not being '100% original'?

B: [*Considers the question*] It's like a kind of perfectionism.

W: Your body is no longer perfect but you believe that it should be?

B: It's not perfect, of course. But yes, that's it.

W: So it seems as if the problem is connected with your expectation of perfection. We haven't really uncovered this expectation yet but it seems to be a burden for you.

Brigitte's problem with the hip operation is reduced to her perceived need – her wish – for a perfect body. This need contains elements of a belief, a desire, and a value, and it contributes to her emotional distress. I can now proceed from the hypothesis that lessening Brigitte's need for perfection will in turn lessen her worry about the operation. Her wish for a perfect body is causing her to suffer.

Physical symptoms caused by injuries

A special case applies when a client's physical symptom is related to a past physical injury. These symptoms can be reduced if energy structures of the injury-causing objects are removed from the client's body or personal space. Such an application is covered in the next case study.

Case study: Joachim

Joachim was in a car accident three years ago. He's now attending one of my seminars. I work with him to neutralise distressing aspects of the trauma, e.g. the images of the car racing towards him, the squealing of the brakes, the sense of panic that he felt when the car hit. Joachim is pleased with the results but says that he would be even happier if I could also remove the pain that he's experienced in his right leg ever since the accident. I give him just two sentences:

- *I retrieve all my energy bound up in the bumper of this car and take it back to the right place in my Self.*
- *I remove all the energy of this bumper from all my cells, from my body and from my personal space, and I send it to where it truly belongs.*

The experiment is a success. Joachim's chronic pain disappears within minutes. I'm still in touch with him several years later, and the pain has never returned.

Chapter 15 in brief:

- Memories, fantasies, and beliefs are elements of experience; representations of a real or virtual world.

- Logosynthesis views these representations as energy structures in space. The representations support the fulfilment of a person's life task if the person is in contact with Essence.

- The representations trigger suffering – distressing physical, emotional, cognitive, and behavioural reactions – if they're frozen and the person isn't in contact with Essence.

---

16 Puzzle pieces II: the reactions

THE PREVIOUS CHAPTER COVERED TRIGGERS' BUILDING BLOCKS: FROZEN MEMORIES, FANTASIES, AND BELIEFS. Triggers are closely entangled with frozen reactions, which are also built up of various elements: physical feelings, emotions, and thoughts. This chapter examines reactions in detail.

Physical feelings

People who haven't learnt to express their needs in a safe and controlled environment can only act and react through their bodies. Someone who has needs that aren't met will often feel tension and limitations within their body. Perception of certain body parts can even be cut off entirely in extreme instances, as in cases of physical or sexual abuse.

We explore physical feelings in Logosynthesis by using meta-question A (as covered in Chapter 11). These physical signs of suffering are multi-layered and can appear during sessions as pressure, headaches, nausea, stomach cramps, shoulder pain, a racing heart, sweating, or cold hands. We don't generally focus on these symptoms; they're instead addressed implicitly in the third Logosynthesis sentence. Symptoms that can disturb sessions (e.g. nausea, dizziness, headaches) will often disappear as suddenly as they appeared if the client drinks a glass of water.

Emotions

We humans have developed survival systems over the course of our evolution that allow us to rapidly process information from our environments. These systems are what we now know as emotions. Emotions are an essential part of the human experience and help us to maintain societal norms and values, make decisions, and act appropriately when we interact with others. We influence other people through our emotions and their emotions also influence us.

Two types of emotions are important in Logosynthesis:

→ Real emotions: direct, appropriate reactions to actual events

→ Archaic emotions: frozen reaction patterns that are connected to memories, fantasies, and beliefs.

Real emotions don't need processing. Life energy flows freely within these emotions and they're appropriate reactions to actual events. Fear is a sensible reaction if three sinister men start following you down a dark street, and this emotion works to prepare your body for running away as fast as possible. Archaic emotions, on the other hand, have lost their original functions through dissociative processes. Energy is bound up within these emotions and they primarily serve our senses of inner stability. Anxiety, mistrust, nostalgia, rage, grief, and shame are all archaic emotions that aren't based on actual events and are instead entangled with memories, fantasies, and beliefs.

It can be difficult to tell whether an emotion is real. Archaic emotions are energy structures that *feel* as if they're connected to your actual environment. If you have a phobia of lifts, for instance, the fear that you feel when you enter a lift is real. If you don't have this phobia then you can't understand how lifts can make someone feel so scared. Applying Logosynthesis is sometimes the only way of discovering whether an emotion is real or archaic. Real emotions remain relevant and present after the Logosynthesis sentences have been applied. Archaic emotions have their energy released by the Logosynthesis sentences, leaving only reactions that are relevant to your environment:

→ Anxiety becomes caution in the face of actual risks and dangers

→ Nostalgia becomes healthy grief for real losses

- Rage becomes self-confidence and the ability to set limits
- Shame becomes a normal level of respect for societal customs
- Mistrust becomes the ability to take a cautious stance in your interactions with others.

Logosynthesis dissolves frozen connections to the past and restores emotions' original functions.

Thoughts

Thoughts that result from triggers often lead to childlike, almost magical conclusions. Children can't assess situations fully and instead reach simplified understandings that are based on their levels of cognitive development.

I spent time with some friends at a castle in small French village while I wrote this book. One morning at breakfast I announced with some pride: 'I've already written four pages today.' A female friend replied: 'Do I have to feel bad about myself now?' My statement had seemingly activated a belief in her about what she should achieve – leading her to think aloud and reach an immediate, distressing conclusion.

Chapter 16 in brief:

- A client's suffering is identified in meta-question A.
- Suffering exists as physical feelings, emotions, and thoughts.
- Suffering is a reaction to representations of memories, fantasies, and beliefs.

---

17 Planning your interventions: Logosynthesis' stages

LOGOSYNTHESIS REQUIRES PROFESSIONALS AND THEIR CLIENTS TO BECOME INVOLVED IN AN UNUSUAL PROCESS AND OBSERVE ITS EFFECTS FROM A CERTAIN INNER DISTANCE. The process can be challenging for both parties regardless of their experience with the method.

The psychologist Robert Yourell wrote an excellent essay on developmental stages in guided change.[60] I've rewritten and extended these five stages for Logosynthesis so that you can see how people's attitudes to the approach can alter. The stages are:

- Caught in resistance
- Ambivalence
- The dark night
- Light at the end of the tunnel
- Essence takes over.

This chapter describes how the five stages are relevant in Logosynthesis. It also clarifies the points that professionals should emphasise with their clients at each level.

[60]Yourell, R. (1998). Levels of Consciousness in Psychotherapy.
URL: www.psychinnovations.com/levels.html.

Stage 1: Caught in resistance

The client reacts immediately and superficially at this stage. Second order dissociation still functions for avoiding archaic pain and there's no motivation to become involved in deep change. The client experiences symptoms as annoying and fails to reflect on his own contributions to the symptoms having appeared.

Rationalisation and a focus on everyday matters are used to provide stability. The client denies the existence of deeper problems, becomes lost in details, and experiences similar reactions over and over again. Emotions seem to be barely differentiated. Anger and irritation are more prominent that anxiety, grief, or despair.

Examples of statements:

- *It doesn't really matter if I have a few drinks now and then*
- *I'll never let her go until she explains why she left me.*

Points of emphasis at this level for professionals:

- Contact – building a solid working relationship
- Understanding how life's pain can manifest as symptoms
- Understanding the client and his inadequate behaviours
- Providing information about solutions and how change occurs
- Concluding initial agreements with a simple phrase: 'Let's confront this and we'll find a solution.'

No concrete strategies are introduced at this stage because their effects would simply evaporate. Introducing Logosynthesis remains out of the question. The client lives in accordance with rigid patterns and lacks the insight and inner stability that are necessary for deep change.

Stage 2: Ambivalence

The client's ambivalence now surfaces and his emotions become more intense. The illusion that everything would be fine if the symptoms disappeared no longer exists; the client now becomes the problem. An increase occurs in the distress that's caused by symptoms (or by the outside world's reactions to symptoms). The client reacts in a more differentiated way but remains stuck in the archaic patterns of Steve Karpman's drama triangle – Victim, Rescuer, Persecutor.[61] Anger gives way to helplessness and anxiety during sessions, but others are still made responsible for the client's suffering.

Example of a statement:

→ *I fought the urge but ended up gambling away $1,000 yesterday. It almost killed me.*

Points of emphasis at this level for professionals:

→ Careful diagnosis and mirroring of avoidance strategies

→ Initial identification and highlighting of the client's own resources

→ Strengthening the working relationship by extending empathy and understanding to intense emotions and the painful status quo (including the client's wish to avoid this status quo)

→ First interpretation of dissociation mechanisms that result from traumatic experiences.

Possible topics to treat with Logosynthesis become clearer at this stage. The client's motivation to find real answers increases. Logosynthesis sentences can be carefully placed to cope with intense emotions in the moment – creating a space for reflection about one's behaviour and experiences. This reflection opens access to deeper layers of consciousness.

Stage 3: The dark night

The client now becomes aware of deeper emotions and motives. He discovers how archaic memories trigger actual experiences, he learns to identify deeper problems, and he recognises avoidance behaviour. An authentic motivation for change and development emerges alongside an

[61]Karpman, S. (1968). Fairy Tales and Script Drama Analysis. Transactional Analysis Bulletin, 7(26), pp. 39-43.

increasing capacity for self-observation. During sessions the client exhibits pain and intense emotions such as fear, rage, and shame in connection with the past. Present behaviour is appreciated in the context of earlier experiences.

Examples of statements:

- *I'm just starting to realise why I'm so angry*
- *I saw this confrontation coming two weeks ago*
- *I put pressure on my partner so that I wouldn't have to look at myself in the mirror*
- *I've always done it that way.*

Points of emphasis at this level for professionals:

- Strengthened awareness of processes occurring within the client
- Intensified perception of own emotions and bodily sensations triggered by the client
- Encouraging change
- Displaying trust in the notion that change is possible.

Logosynthesis is most effective when it's applied during this stage. The client is able to identify and explore frozen worlds from the past; awareness of dissociative processes lies just beneath the surface. Cognitive and emotional differentiation between past trauma and the present are now possible.

Applying Logosynthesis during this stage makes the application much gentler than is possible in many other models of psychotherapy. Using the sentences rapidly reduces the intensity and threatening nature of emotions, thereby making re-traumatisation rare. The client's capacity for differentiation between past and present is dramatically increased.

Stage 4: Light at the end of the tunnel

New insights now strengthen the client's desire for change. Symptoms' previous meanings dissolve in the active search for the Self and the meaning of life. Symptoms in general become less important. The client's focus shifts to recognising conclusions about life that were reached during early childhood – and replacing these frozen beliefs with newly won insights. The client develops fresh perspectives and actively takes on responsibility in the counselling process. A new and focused interest in the environment starts to surface, along with awareness of the contexts in which people inflicted past suffering. The client's body becomes more relaxed as facial expressions, breathing patterns, and postures change. These changes are observed with joy and relief.

Examples of statements:

→ *My teacher was wrong. It's destructive to humiliate children in front of their entire class.*

→ *I can now see that my husband abused me and that the roots of this abuse lay in his childhood.*

Points of emphasis at this level for professionals:

→ First experiences of complete physical relaxation

→ Intensified perception of the body

→ Initial notion of a positive physical state as an alternative to conventional physical reactions

→ Spontaneous, adult insights into complex conditions and causes

→ Strengthening the working relationship

→ Engaging the client's own potential in the change process.

Logosynthesis is also highly effective when it's applied during this stage. The client can neutralise every block on his path without feeling overwhelmed; frozen worlds collapse like dominoes. The client starts to enjoy this developmental process and works between sessions on dissolving blocked emotions, beliefs, memories, and behaviour patterns. This is where self-coaching comes in. The meta-questions and Logosynthesis sentences become so familiar that the professional's presence is no longer required for their application.

Stage 5: Essence takes over

The client now recognises his worth and this knowledge spreads into other areas of his life. A deep sense of relaxation sets in on an everyday basis. Symptoms lose their relevance and past pains no longer play a role in day-to-day living. The client revises relationship patterns, either breaking off or renewing old relationships or initiating new relationships. People who caused pain are understood and forgiven.

Examples of statements:

- *I don't have to achieve anything to be respected as a human being*
- *I had no idea that I was so wound up*
- *My parents couldn't act any differently. Their own experiences were no different and they were simply overwhelmed.*

Points of emphasis at this level for professionals:

- Exploration and implementation of alternatives to inadequate previous patterns
- Reflection on new experiences
- Consideration to expanding network of relationships
- Finding a new language for the achievement and experience of change
- Bringing in the harvest!

Logosynthesis is restricted to picking up the pieces during this stage. A client who reaches this stage reassesses his goals and looks at what's left to work through. Momentary physical experiences, emotions, thoughts, and beliefs are explored with the same intentions. Perceived blocks to these goals are dissolved. The focus shifts from past problems to the meaning and purpose of life. Self-coaching with Logosynthesis is possible for many issues.

Logosynthesis as an everyday practice

A sixth stage can be added to Robert Yourell's essay in the context of Logosynthesis applications: using the model every day. A client who's able to apply Logosynthesis every day will retrieve and remove energy as a routine, in turn dramatically increasing his quality of life.

There are many reasons for regularly using Logosynthesis, including to prevent small, unexpressed irritations, and to master the fact that the world is less than perfect. Limiting beliefs no longer stand in the way, relationships improve, and thoughts become clearer. Logosynthesis becomes a toothbrush for the soul, and the only challenge becomes the future.

Chapter 17 in brief:

- Logosynthesis distinguishes five stages of development.
- Logosynthesis can't be applied while the client resists.
- Logosynthesis can be introduced when ambivalence surfaces.
- Logosynthesis' full power can unfold when the client becomes fully conscious of a problem.
- The client can take over responsibility for the Logosynthesis process once light appears at the end of the tunnel.
- Logosynthesis can be pursued as a daily practice once awareness of Essence begins to replace disturbing patterns.

---

18 Exploring space and time: timelines and maps

IN THIS CHAPTER I INTRODUCE TWO METHODS THAT CAN HELP CLIENTS TO DEEPEN AND INTENSIFY THEIR LOGOSYNTHESIS WORK. These methods are 'Timelines' and 'Personal Space Mapping' (or 'Mapping' for short).

Timelines

Timelines help people to explore, activate and neutralise blocks in their pasts and futures. The method was developed by NLP author and trainer Robert Dilts and extended by Tad James.[62]

Using timelines requires time and trust. I schedule at least 90 minutes for these sessions because the approach can easily activate many levels of unknown trauma. The process is faster in groups but a minimum of one hour is always required. Your clients also need to trust you. It's impossible to predict what the method will uncover, so clients may need to rely on your support at any point. Stay close and guard their personal spaces from just outside their fields of vision, being wary not to cross their timelines yourself.

---

[62]James, T. & Woodsmall, W. (1988). Time Line Therapy and the Basis of Personality. Meta Publications.

Timelines into the past

Timelines into the past help people to identify and neutralise traumatic prior events. These timelines are especially useful when clients have carried disturbing topics with them for long periods.

You work with timelines into the past as follows:

- Identify a painful experience or symptom. Explore this experience or symptom with the help of meta-question A and let the client give it a number from 0 to 10 on the SUD scale (Subjective Units of Distress).
- Clear a space that's at least two or three metres wide around your client. A six to eight metre space is even better.
- Give the client a marker such as a pebble or piece of card. Ask him to place this marker somewhere in the space to anchor the present.
- Stay close to the client but don't enter his space and avoid making direct eye contact.
- Ask the client to place another marker in the space to represent the beginning of life. Now invite the client to stand on the 'Present' spot.
- Ask the client to become aware of the painful experience or symptom. When he feels it, tell him to move backwards towards the 'Beginning of life' marker.
- As the client moves, ask him to look for moments when he felt the experience or symptom. Request that he stops on the timeline whenever such a moment is discovered.
- Whenever the client stops, invite him to describe the moment as if it were happening now. Ask questions such as 'How are you?', 'What's happening?' and 'Who's there?' The client's answers will provide the material for meta-question B.
- Mark the position of each stop with another anchor. Ask the client if that event was the origin of his experience or symptom.
- If the client says that it was, clarify the situation with the meta-questions and neutralise it with the three sentences. If the client says that the experience or symptom existed before the event, ask him to continue going back in time.

- Many of the moments are likely to be dramatic. They'll be characterised by abandonment, violence, and lack of love. Remember that these memories and reactions are simply frozen energy structures that can be neutralised – even though they may seem extremely real.

- It's not uncommon for clients to uncover traumas from very early childhood or before birth. You may even find that events surface from a client's past lives, traces of which still burden the person in the present.

- When the client has identified and neutralised the first distressing experience or symptom, invite him to move back along the timeline towards the 'Present' marker.

- On the way towards this marker, the client will encounter the more recent experiences of the emotion or symptom and explore whether distress still exists.

- Work through any moments that are still distressing with the Logosynthesis sentences.

- Upon returning to the 'Present' marker, the client compares the level of distress with the level at the start of the exercise. Use this response to determine whether the session can be ended.

Case study: Helen

Helen is a 40 year-old businesswoman who's come to me in a state of distress. Her boss, her most important and trusted colleague, has recently left the firm. She now isn't sure if she can keep her job. She also has no idea how to apply her recent professional training in the workplace. She tells me that she feels as if the ground is slipping away beneath her feet, and this description strikes me as important.

I ask Helen to stand in a space and focus on the sensation of the ground slipping away. I ask her to place markers within the space for all the times she experienced this feeling from her birth to the present day. She initially identifies two events: the separation from her husband seven years ago and her parents' separation when she was ten years old. When she goes back even further she discovers the same feeling at her birth. She came into the world and felt completely abandoned. I now ask her to lengthen the timeline and look further back, right to the moment of conception. She discovers a sensation that's completely new to her: looking forward to life. We discover that the feeling of the ground slipping away originated during the second trimester of the pregnancy. Her mother had become pregnant with her lover and the discovery of the pregnancy had caused her considerable distress.

I now ask Helen to find an image of her pregnant mother in my consulting room. I then give her three sentences for this image. Helen calms down after the first cycle; the feeling of the ground slipping has faded and she feels joy about the life that she's about to enter. We carry on working towards the present. She encounters no problems during her entry into the world and she goes on to experience her parents' divorce with greater calm. She's sad at first, but this emotion dissipates when we work on the unfulfilled wish that her parents would remain together. We work through her divorce in the same way. An unfulfilled desire becomes the topic for the Logosynthesis sentences – this time the desire to overcome the differences that exist between her and her husband. When we finally return to the here-and-now point on the timeline, Helen's experience of the ground slipping away beneath her feet has completely vanished.

We spend the final part of our session on Helen's decision to give up or keep her job. She projects the timeline into the future and explores both possible scenarios. She views the options in a relaxed manner, although with a slight preference for keeping her job.

Timelines into the future

You can also use timelines to relieve distress about the future. You work with timelines into the future as follows:

- The client picks a spot in space to signify the present moment.
- Anchor this spot with a sheet of paper. Write 'F°' on this sheet; 'F' stands for 'Future'.
- Ask the client to stand on the spot. Now explore the present with the question, 'What do you want to change in your life?'
- Ask the client to find the direction of the future on the timeline.

- Ask the client to look into the future and find a point on the future timeline at which the goal has been reached. Mark this spot as 'F^1.'
- Ask the client to go and stand at this point.
- The client now explores what it feels like to have reached the goal and what life looks like in terms of work, relationships, health, or finances.
- Invite the client to look back towards the 'Present' spot from this point. Ask questions such as: 'What happens when you look at your younger Self?', 'How does it feel to have made it?', and 'What steps did you take to get here?'
- Have the client return to the 'Present' spot.
- Ask the client to again move towards the future point – this time very slowly, paying attention to changes in bodily feelings and emotions.
- Ask the client to stop on the timeline whenever he experiences hesitation or a block.
- If the client stops, explore the thoughts and fantasies that led to the hesitation or block as well as the reactions to these thoughts and fantasies, i.e. meta-questions A and B.
- Now apply Logosynthesis to the hesitation or block.
- Ask the client to proceed slowly again once the hesitation or block has been neutralised. Explore, identify, and neutralise any other hesitations or blocks that are encountered on the way to the future spot.
- Have the client reach the future spot, return to the present, and then make the trip again. Repeat this process several times until the walk is completely smooth.
- Invite the client to return to the 'Present' point and look into the future once again. Ask, 'When, where, and with whom will you do this?' Let the client send you an email once these resolutions have been turned into realities.

A variation of the timelines into the future exercise involves working with the fulfilment of a client's life mission. F^1 is now the moment at which the client leaves the Earth and looks back at his life. What's been fulfilled? What obstacles did he overcome? These obstacles are then identified and neutralised on the timeline.

The use of timelines in Logosynthesis feels very natural. The free flow of life energy activates the client's entire potential. In contrast to NLP, the client takes no meta-positions beside the timeline and doesn't consciously activate specific resources from the past. Essence remains the ultimate resource.

Personal Space Mapping

Personal Space Mapping is another tool that can be used to investigate complex energy structures and then dissolve these structures in a step-by-step manner. Mapping activates relevant introjects in the client's personal space. The introjects are then marked on the floor with paper sheets, pebbles, coins, or wooden figures. All distressing dissociative structures can be identified, located, and neutralised successively once such a map has been created. Mapping is especially suited to work in groups, but it can also be used in individual sessions if a double session is booked.

Be aware that mapping can be very intense. It demands a lot of energy and concentration from both the client and you as the professional. Stay close to the client while taking care not to step into the space that's occupied by his map.

You work with mapping as follows:

→ The client finds a spot on an imaginary map to represent the current situation. The map exists on the floor within the client's personal space.

→ Find an actual or historical situation that causes emotional distress. This can be a present situation, e.g. training for a new job, or a situation from family history.

→ Identify significant people, themes, and objects in the situation. These are all placed on the map. Important people who are deceased can also be given places on the map. The client now has a representation of the whole situation that includes all of the actors.

→ Invite the client to walk around the entire map and make improvements if necessary.

You have two options for working with distressing relationships once a clear map has been achieved:

→ You begin with the least distressing relationships and so release energy for dealing with the more distressing relationships. Small, early successes empower the client in his confrontations with the most potent introjects.

→ You begin with the most distressing relationships. This variation requires adequate strength and also sufficient trust in the working relationship.

The next decision involves the choice of positions and roles:

→ Once the client has chosen a first relationship to focus on, explore the positions of the actors involved. Many variations are possible, e.g. the relationship with a parent from the client's position, the relationship with a parent from the parent's position, or even the relationships between the clients' parents.

→ Evaluate the distress of the person involved in each position. Prompt a short interview between the relevant actors. The interview should be long enough for the suffering to come alive. The client should also assess the SUD scores.

→ The client now says the sentences from the chosen position. The focus of each sentence is always 'this perception of you,' along with the relevant actor's name:

> **1** *I retrieve all my energy bound up in this perception of you, (name), and take it back to the right place in my Self.*

> **2** *I remove all non-me energy bound up with this perception of you, (name), from my cells, from my body, and my personal space, and I send it to where it truly belongs.*

> **3** *I retrieve all my energy bound up in all my reactions to this perception of you, (name), and take it back to the right place in my Self.*

→ The client continues to neutralise one relationship after another. Change the direction or focus on another actor if a particular relationship's distress level can't be reduced.

- Other actors may appear during the process. These actors also receive positions on the map. This often happens with deceased family members or people who have left an organisation.

- Let the client remove the markers of any people who no longer trigger distress.

After clearing a relationship, the client returns to the starting position and explores the distress that's now present within the situation. Explore the tension between the representations of the people on the map, and then initiate another cycle for the actor who subsequently causes the most distress.

The mapping ends:

- If the session has to finish because of time constraints. Identify unresolved topics to carry over to the next session.

- When the level of distress associated with the situation has reached an acceptable level.

- When the client's personal space is cleared of all representations of people, objects, and themes.

The last option is the best from a Logosynthesis perspective, as the cleared space allows the client an unclouded perception of people and events in the present. This total clearance is a realistic goal in advanced coaching and psychotherapy processes.

I always make the end of mapping sessions a ritual by asking clients to collect the markers and decide what to do with them. Some simply throw them into the waste paper bin while others take them home to dispose of or explore further.

Case study: Carola

Carola is a 47 year-old consultant who's recently become self-employed. She comes to me complaining of a lack of support in her new venture. My follow-up questions soon reveal that her problem is really about her husband, although she's previously felt the same lack of support from her sister and mother. I give Carola some coloured cards and ask her to choose different colours for different people: her husband; her mother; and her sister. She also chooses cards to represent herself and her new professional status. I now ask her to use the cards to build a map within her personal space. She slowly paces around, putting the cards on the floor and making corrections until the task is complete. All of the cards lie very close together.

I ask Carola to stand on her own card and explore the actor with whom she experiences the most pressure or tension. This turns out to be her mother. I ask her to move to her mother's position and consider the situation from there. She tells me – as her mother – how proud she is of her daughter and how much she wants to support her. I give her three Logosynthesis sentences that include the subject: 'this perception of you, Carola,' and then ask her to return to her own position on the map. Her relationship with her mother is now neutral. I invite her to update the map to reflect this change and she moves her mother's marker much further away.

Carola's next source of tension lies in her relationship with her sister. I ask her to take up her sister's position on the map. It quickly becomes clear that her sister envies her a great deal because of her marriage, family, education, and profession. I have Carola say the sentences with the subject: 'this perception of you, Carola.' When she returns to her own position, the pressure between her and her sister is gone. The updated map shows a greater distance between Carola and her sister, as well.

The final relationship is the one with her husband. When she's neutralised his representation she repositions the cards once more, this time placing the card for her professional independence on top of the card for herself. Her original distress is gone. Carola's final action is to pick up the cards and carefully pack them away as precious souvenirs.

Mapping and Family Constellations

Personal Space Mapping may seem familiar to professionals who are know the Family Constellations work of figures such as Bert Hellinger[63] and Matthias Varga von Kibed.[64] Both methods require clients to create representations of their material and social environments in space, but three significant differences exist between the approaches:

- Family Constellations requires other people to substitute for the client or take on the positions of introjects in the client's space. Mapping doesn't make use of other people in the client's personal space.

- Mapping only uses the Logosynthesis sentences to neutralise disturbing relationships or traumatic events.

- Mapping only resolves blocks by moving energy to and from the client's position. The content of messages is never reframed and there's no explicit acknowledgement of other people's meanings or roles in the processing work. A client's frame of reference changes automatically when the relevant energy has been retrieved and removed.

Mapping is especially suitable for the clarification of complex situations and invisible loyalties.[65] Clients are often driven by diffuse introjects. Mapping can help to differentiate and subsequently dissolve disturbing emotions, e.g. guilt associated with divorce or death, or anxiety adopted from parents or grandparents. Family Constellation work can also help with these areas, but the work is much more gentle and efficient in Logosynthesis. Logosynthesis sees the material processed directly in the amygdala without the content of the client's experience being actively reframed.

[63]Hellinger, B. (2003). Ordnungen des Helfens. Ein Schulungsbuch. Heidelberg: Carl-Auer.

[64]Varga von Kibéd, M. & Sparrer, I. (2005). Ganz im Gegenteil, Tetralemma-Arbeit und andere Grundformen Systemischer Strukturaufstellungen.

[65]Boszormeny-Nagy, I. & Spark, G. (1984). Invisible Loyalties: Reciprocity in Intergenerational Family Therapy. Brunner-Mazel; Reprint edition.

Case study: Kim

The mapping technique can also be used to integrate split parts within a person. The person identifies parts or extreme positions, finds a new, neutral spot in the room, and then occupies this spot as a starting point for integration. The technique is covered in detail during the Institute's training seminars and requires careful preparation and follow-up. This case study has been included only to make you aware of the tool's potential.

17 year-old Kim is about to realise her dream of being cast in a theatrical production. She ultimately wants to become an actress and director, but a nervous tic in the corner of her eye threatens her ambition. The tic only appears when she's excited, but it's been enough to reduce her chances of being cast in the past. The problem distresses her a great deal.

I explore the issue with Kim and soon find that two parts are involved in her distress. One part wants a career in the theatre while the other part doesn't agree with this ambition at all. I ask Kim to find a place in the room for each part and to mark these places. I then turn to each part and interview it. The aspiring actress emphasises how important casting is to her, but the other part – the part with the tic – feels that she should take a more 'normal' path. Both parts are equally stubborn and refuse to recognise the other's good intentions.

I ask Kim to find a third place in the room from which she can see both parts at a distance. She becomes much calmer as soon as she finds this spot. I then have her address both parts with the three Logosynthesis sentences. Her distress continues to reduce and she finally says: 'It doesn't matter if I don't get a role this time. There'll be many more opportunities in the future.'

Chapter 18 in brief:

- Timelines and Personal Space Mapping are effective techniques for deepening a client's work with Logosynthesis.

- Both techniques primarily serve to clarify the client's situation.

- Distressing themes are neutralised with the three Logosynthesis sentences once a situation has been depicted in time or space.

- Both techniques avoid interpretations, judgments, reframing, and other types of cognitive restructuring. The three Logosynthesis sentences alter a client's frame of reference without content being offered by the accompanying professional.

19 Useful tips

THIS CHAPTER FEATURES USEFUL TIPS THAT WILL HELP YOU TO APPLY LOGOSYNTHESIS IN YOUR PRACTICE. The tip headings are as follows:

- Energy, not psychology
- Slow down and dismantle stress
- Go backwards in time
- Signals of addiction
- Logosynthesis with God's help
- All the sentences every time?
- Staying in control
- The plate warmer: does it ever stop?

Please remember that Logosynthesis is still being developed and new aspects are being discovered on a regular basis. The only way to stay up-to-date with the latest tips is through continued training at the Institute.

Energy, not psychology

Many professionals are very good at understanding their clients' needs. Your experiences with Logosynthesis will gradually shift your focus away from these needs and onto what activates them. Logosynthesis is the study of the energetic structure of subjective experience, i.e. its form and not its content. If you focus on this structure, you don't need to pay attention to content; energy flows freely or is blocked, and either belongs to the client or doesn't. With practice you'll eventually come to understand your clients' statements as energy structure descriptions.

Slow down and dismantle stress

Many clients only turn to counselling or psychotherapy when second order dissociation fails, i.e. they can no longer avoid their problems by eating, drinking, smoking, gambling, or working. You can try to repair a client's defence mechanisms, but this will only rarely lead to success and will only work in part when it *is* successful. The solution is to slow down the process.

Create an environment in which clients can lower their stress levels to the point that first order dissociation can surface, i.e. trauma, grief, failure, abandonment. These feelings interrupt contact with Essence, but Logosynthesis can resolve first order dissociation. Healing the interruption not only re-establishes contact with Essence – it also decreases the necessity of second and third order dissociation to suppress the old pain.

Go backwards in time

A person suffers because life energy has split off from the Original Self in reaction to traumatic events. The split-off energy from each event builds structures that can be activated at any time. These structures in turn trigger emotions, thoughts, and forms of behaviour that are similar to the person's initial reaction to the associated traumatic event.

A traumatic event can lie a long way back in the past. I recommend neutralising the earliest memories and fantasies if possible – provided you're trained to do this and you can do it within your practice framework. Most triggers originate in early childhood, although it's not uncommon for traumas to surface that can only be understood in the context of a person's birth or time in the womb. Stanislav Grof's Basal Perinatal Matrices (BPM) model has proven useful for understanding the application of Logosynthesis to these earlier periods.[66]

[66]Grof, S. (1998). Human nature and the nature of reality: conceptual challenges from consciousness research. Journal of Psychoactive Drugs. Vol. 30, No. 4.

Many clients go even further back and report traumatic death, loss, and abandonment events from past lives. The work of shaman Sandra Ingerman refers to such issues.[67] Applying Logosynthesis to these cases is the same as working with any other kind of frozen energy structure, although preparing for and following up on this kind of trauma processing is especially important. Further details on this topic are beyond the scope of this book and form part of the Institute's advanced training programme for professionals.

Signals of addiction

Addiction is a form of second order dissociation. It serves state management, i.e. the stabilisation of the client's inner and outer condition and the avoidance of existential abandonment. Taking away the substance or activity brings a person into contact with this abandonment. Addiction treatment often tries to overcome withdrawal symptoms with substitute substances or 'toughing it out' with other people's help. Logosynthesis takes a different direction and aims to make the symptoms irrelevant by working on underlying hurt – the avoidance of which was the addiction's original function.

I use a special technique called the 'key signal' when I work with addiction. The key signal is a physical symptom or signal that the addict experiences and that's immediately connected with his need for the substance or activity. The addict wouldn't need the substance or activity if this key signal didn't exist, but it's so powerful that he has no choice but to reach for the substance or activity when it's activated. Smokers often find the signal to be a pulling sensation at the top of their sternums. Many Logosynthesis cycles are generally required before the craving for a cigarette disappears completely; the addiction is rooted in numerous events in which the client has been abandoned or ignored, and all of these events first need to be neutralised.

---

[67]Ingerman, S. (1991). Soul Retrieval: Mending the Fragmented Self. San Francisco: Harper.

Logosynthesis with God's help

People with strict religious worldviews often find the idea of words having power to border on arrogance or even blasphemy. My task with Logosynthesis is to lessen suffering, so I don't discuss religious beliefs with my clients. Religious clients can find the Logosynthesis experience less threatening if they say the sentences with the addition, 'with God's help':[68]

1   *With God's help I retrieve all my energy bound up in X and take it back to the right place in my Self.*

2   *With God's help I remove all non-me energy in connection with X from all my cells, from my body and out of my personal space, and I send it to where it truly belongs.*

3   *With God's help I retrieve all my energy bound up in all my reactions to X and take it back to the right place in my Self.*

All the sentences every time?

It's always best to use all three sentences if someone is new to Logosynthesis – and to follow these with the fourth sentence when the work is completely finished. The client can then learn the effect of a complete cycle in a step-by-step way. It may seem that the client's distress level has reduced to a zero after only the first or second sentences, but a deepening of the effect is often still possible. Reaction patterns have been practised for years and bind far more energy than many people think.

You'll sometimes find that the first sentence causes the surfacing of material that's older, more distressing, or more clearly differentiated. It's wise to repeat the first sentence if this occurs, but based on the recovered sensory perceptions and never with emotions! Explore whether the initial material is neutral once you've processed the new frozen perceptions. Complete another cycle if there's still work to do.

---

[68] I wish to extend my thanks to my colleague Peter Haas for this idea.

Staying in control

Many counselling professionals are trained to offer considerable space to their clients' emotions. The emotions are often described in great detail and the professionals learn to provide empathetic support. Modern society also encourages people to identify with their emotions and view them almost as possessions that are worth protecting. Logosynthesis takes a different approach: you don't need any emotions that are triggered by frozen memories, fantasies, or beliefs.

Working with meta-question A requires you to take a client's emotions seriously. This action strengthens your working relationship and increases your credibility as a professional. Nevertheless, you actively switch to meta-question B as soon as you know what the client is suffering from. Meta-question B is where you take the lead, as the client won't usually be aware of the triggers that meta-question B uncovers.

It's also important for you to take the lead during the processing phase after the sentences have been spoken. A client may react to a sentence with intense emotions, but your task is simply to offer the next sentence – knowing that the client's pain is archaic and will lessen with that next sentence. Clear structure confirms the working relationship far better than sympathetic mirroring or interpretation of the client's experience.

The client's amygdala similarly understands clearly formulated imperatives; evolution has ensured that children obey their parents in case of danger. Overly polite forms of the sentences should therefore be avoided. 'Would you like to say this sentence?' asks for a decision and so unnecessarily activates the frontal lobe. This is counterproductive as Logosynthesis only works on the level of the limbic system. The better, clearer form is: 'Now say the following sentence.' In time you can simply present the sentences with an intonation that makes clear that you expect the client to repeat them.

The plate warmer: does it ever stop?

There comes a point in most Logosynthesis applications when the client discovers that using the method can make disturbing memories, fantasies, and beliefs disappear. This discovery provides relief, but the next discovery is often that new, unknown memories are soon to surface. The subconscious mind has repressed these memories for many years so as to protect the client in his everyday life, and it keeps on delivering new material once it knows how to process the images. This can be distressing.

I call this loop the 'plate warmer' effect. Think of a plate warmer in a restaurant. When a waiter removes a hot plate, the next one automatically takes its place. The machine looks exactly the same from the outside after each plate has been taken away. It's the same with the client's emotions: they feel the same even though the trigger is different. If clients are discouraged by this plate warmer effect, they need time to explore the differences between the triggers and the similarity of their reactions. Such integration helps clients to see what's changed in their lives as a result of Logosynthesis. It's also worth emphasising that Logosynthesis is an on-going process with on-going results; every single application deepens a client's awareness of Essence and so has a positive effect on the present and the future.

Chapter 19 in brief:

- This chapter contains a series of useful tips that concern the application of the Logosynthesis basic procedure.

PART III

LOGOSYNTHESIS LIVE: A GLANCE OVER MY SHOULDER

Introduction

LOGOSYNTHESIS' EFFECTIVENESS IS ALREADY CLEAR TO HUNDREDS OF PRACTITIONERS, BUT ITS CLAIMS AREN'T YET SUPPORTED BY SCIENTIFIC RESEARCH. The mainstream perspective views the practitioners' experiences as merely a series of anecdotes that may form the basis for future research. I want to present my work with Logosynthesis in a transparent way that speeds up potential research, so this section contains video and audio transcripts from my practice and Logosynthesis training sessions. The method's power becomes really clear over the following chapters.

I've shortened the transcripts – except Claudio's in Chapter 21 – to increase readability and emphasise the key concepts. Repetition and less relevant comments have been excluded. The editing of the text hasn't cut any of the transitions, however. Some changes may seem improbably fast, but this is due to Logosynthesis' effects. Working with Logosynthesis gives rise to two types of transition that don't occur in other counselling models:

→ The client often shows intense emotional reactions after he pauses for the effects of the first and second sentences. The professional doesn't react explicitly to these reactions but instead goes on to the next sentence – secure in the knowledge that the emotional charge will be lessened when the next sentence is said.

→ After the third sentence, and often earlier, the client's distress level is dramatically lessened through the effects of the power of the word.

My commentary (in italic print) relates to aspects of the model and its methods that are covered elsewhere in this book. The clients' statements are always introduced with the first letter of their names, e.g. 'A' for 'Alec.' My own statements are introduced with a 'W' for 'Willem.'

All of the transcripts convince me of Logosynthesis' simplicity, efficiency, and extensive possibilities.

20 Alec: I'll never amount to anything

ALEC PARTICIPATES IN A LOGOSYNTHESIS LIVE SEMINAR. One of the first things he says when we meet is, 'I'll never amount to anything.' This belief has limited his career progress for a long time. Our session lasts for 34 minutes.

W: Alec, what's your theme?

A: 'I'll never amount to anything.'

W: This sounds like a conclusion that's based on experience.

A: *[Hesitant]* Yes. I confirm this conclusion time and time again.

W: How do you do that?

A: I never finish anything.

W: How old are you?

A: 44.

W: How long have you known the theme sentence: 'I'll never amount to anything'?

A: My mother mentioned something when my career was first starting to take off. She told me that one of my aunts had once said: 'He'll never amount to anything.' The notion seemed familiar to me. This was the first time that I knew the sentence in a concrete form, but the feeling has been there for longer.

W: When did your aunt say that?

A: My mother told me about it when I was 21, but my aunt had said it 5-8 years earlier.

W: What happens when you think of the sentence? What emotions or physical sensations do you experience? Let's try right now: 'He'll never amount to anything.'

A: A sense of resignation sets in. My hands and legs also feel heavy.

W: Go back in time and find out how long you've known resignation and heaviness in your hands and legs. Think about the first time you experienced the feelings and then look for an earlier example.

A: I definitely didn't know the feelings before I was five. Anything was possible back then.

W: Go back to being five years old. You've never heard: 'He'll never amount to anything.' Now close your eyes and go forwards in time until something happens. What is this something?

A: My mother meets her future husband, my stepfather. It wasn't long before I had to leave my grandmother and move in with my stepfather. I remember wanting to go back to my grandmother and realising that everything had changed. My stepfather was also a teacher, and this emphasised all of my weaknesses at school.

W: Was this the first time your hands and legs felt heavy?

A: Yes, but now I'm remembering my first love. It must have happened in first or second grade. I was so surprised that the girl I liked also liked me back. I couldn't believe that someone would take an interest in me.

W: So you must have experienced someone not taking an interest in you. Do you remember grown-ups finding something else more important than you?

A: Yes, when we moved in with my stepfather. Everything felt warm at my grandmother's, but now something was cold. There's a much earlier example, as well: my parents weren't married when I was conceived and my father left soon after he found out that my mother was pregnant. He took no interest in me.

W: Go back and re-experience the moment when your father abandoned you and your mother. You're in your mother's womb and your father leaves. What's happening within you? Don't think. Just pay attention to what happens automatically.

A: I feel fear.

W: Fear of what? Tell me your first thought.

A: Nothing concrete. Perhaps fear of the darkness.

W: I retrieve all my energy *[A repeats]* bound up in this darkness *[A repeats]* and take it back to the right place in my Self *[A repeats]*.

A: *[Closes his eyes and falls silent. He opens his eyes after 52 seconds.]*

W: What's happening now?

A: The fear is still there and its level hasn't changed – but movement is possible.

W: I remove all non-me energy *[A repeats]* in connection with this darkness and fear *[A repeats]* from all my cells, from my body and from my personal space *[A repeats]* and I send it to where it truly belongs *[A repeats]*.

[45 seconds pass]

I retrieve all my energy *[A repeats]* bound up in all my reactions to this darkness *[A repeats]* and take it back to the right place in my Self *[A repeats]*.

Part III ▌ *Logosynthesis live: a glance over my shoulder* 163

A: *[Falls silent for 50 seconds. He then makes eye contact.]*

W: What's going on now?

A: I feel alone.

W: What happens when you're alone? What's the feeling connected to? Where are you now?

A: I think that I'm still in the womb…

W: How many months has your mother been pregnant? Give me your first thought.

A: Four, perhaps five.

W: Explore what's happening. You're alone. What emotions are connected to this state?

A: I long for protection. Everyone's busy with someone else.

W: I retrieve all my energy *[A repeats]* bound up in this idea of protection *[A repeats]* and take it back to the right place in my Self *[A repeats]*.

A: *[Falls silent for 40 seconds. He then makes eye contact.]*

W: I remove all non-me energy *[A repeats]* in connection with this idea of protection *[A repeats]* from all my cells, from my body and from my personal space *[A repeats]* and I send it to where it truly belongs *[A repeats]*.

A: *[Breathes deeply for 40 seconds]* I somehow perceive that I don't want to be born.

W: You don't want to be born.

A: No, I don't.

W: I retrieve all my energy *[A repeats]* bound up in the part of myself that doesn't want to be born *[A repeats]* and take it back to the right place in my Self *[A repeats]*.

A: *[Falls silent for 30 seconds. He then makes eye contact.]*

W: I remove all non-me energy *[A repeats]* in connection with the wish not to be born *[A repeats]* from all my cells, from my body and from my personal space *[A repeats]* and I send it to where it truly belongs *[A repeats]*.

A: *[Falls silent for 50 seconds. He then makes eye contact.]*

W: Okay. I retrieve all my energy *[A repeats]* bound up in all my reactions to this unfulfilled wish of not being born *[A repeats]* and take it back to the right place in my Self *[A repeats]*.

A: *[Falls silent for 55 seconds. He then makes eye contact and sighs.]*

W: What's happening?

A: I feel a mixture of anger and sadness.

W: What makes you angry? What makes you sad?

A: *[Silent for a long time, then coughs]* Nothing concrete. Nothing precise. I might be angry about the circumstances. It's mixed up. I'm angry because I spent four or five years with my grandmother and then lost this home.

W: I retrieve all my energy *[A repeats]* bound up in the impossible alternative *[A repeats]* and take it back to the right place in my Self *[A repeats]*.

A: *[Falls silent for 45 seconds. He then makes eye contact and begins to laugh.]*

W: *[Surprised]* What's up?

A: It's my path. Perhaps it all belongs to my path.

W: Okay. I retrieve all my energy *[A repeats]* bound up in all my reactions to the impossible alternative *[A repeats]* and take it back to the right place in my Self *[A repeats]*.

Part III ⦙ *Logosynthesis live: a glance over my shoulder*   165

A: I'm struggling with the phrase 'the impossible alternative.' I don't know what this is connected to. Can you please say the sentence again?

W: I'd rather go back. Do you still feel grief and anger?

A: No, both feelings are gone. *[Looks at W. Both laugh.]*

W: Go back to the 'He'll never amount to anything' sentence. How is it now? What's happened with this sentence?

A: It's become relative. It's connected to 'It's my path.' I'll amount to something on my path. The sentence doesn't have the power that it had before.

W: How valid was the sentence before on a scale from 0 to 10?

A: 8 to 9.

W: And now?

A: It's still a 3 or 4.

W: Well, you'll never become an astronaut.

A: *[Laughs]* Absolutely not!

W: What else will you never amount to? What will you amount to?

A: It's stupid. The sentence was just in space; it wasn't connected to anything or the idea of some person. I'll amount to what I amount to. I'll amount to what's on my path. It's okay.

W: And apparently you must have chosen this path.

A: *[Laughs]* Yes, I must have.

W: Can we leave it here?

A: Yes.

21 Claudio: doing what needs to be done

CLAUDIO BRINGS UP A PROBLEM DURING A LOGOSYNTHESIS LIVE SEMINAR: HE CAN'T DO WHAT NEEDS TO BE DONE. The session lasts for 35 minutes. The following transcript is unedited.

W: Claudio, what's your topic?

C: I procrastinate constantly with things that I could get done. Some things need time and are a process, but other things could just be done and finished.

W: You say that you could do things.

C: Yes, in theory. When I have to fill out a form, I could either wait until the day of the deadline or I could sit down and do it right away. Then it would be out of the way.

W: What does not doing this say about you?

C: I'm lazy; a lazy bum. Something like that.

W: This sounds more or less like you're being hard on yourself.

C: Yes, there are definitely other ways of working. Ways that you should work. I'm hard on myself because I suffer from the procrastination. I create pressure when I don't act, but I also know how good it feels to have done something. My mother did the same, and she was a much worse procrastinator.

W: Your mother did the same?

C: As I recall, yes.

W: When you say 'I'm a lazy bum,' it sounds to me like someone is angry. It's very different from: 'I approach things in a relaxed way.'

C: Yes. I get angry with myself because I feel as if I could make life much simpler by just doing things.

W: You say: 'I get angry with myself.' Where in space is the part that gets angry? You're splitting yourself into a part that gets angry and a part to get angry at. It sounds like the two parts are in a power struggle, with the passive part showing the active part that it has the power.

C: Yes.

W: The passive part controls the process. The active part has no power to force you to act.

C: Yes, I only act when there's pressure or I have no choice.

W: There's a lot of energy bound up in this dialogue if I'm hearing it correctly.

C: *[Thoughtful]* Sometimes. Sometimes I reach the decision that I won't do something. That choice is fine. It's the struggle that's stressful, the back and forth when I don't make a decision. The fight between the active and passive parts is tiring.

W: Okay.

C: I wish the active part would be stronger – or that I had a choice.

W: Be the passive part. You often put things off. Where in space is the part that gets angry at you?

C: *[Points with his right arm]* Above and to the right.

W: How far away?

C: *[Points again]* It sticks out and then goes down behind my head on the right side. It ends up in my neck.

W: How do you know that this part is angry? Does it say or show something?

C: I see a head that looks angry if I look closely.

W: How distressed are you on a scale from 0 to 10 when the head looks angry?

C: 8.

W: 8. That's high enough *[C smiles]*. Okay. I retrieve all my energy *[C repeats]* bound up in this angry head *[C repeats]* and take it back to the right place in my Self *[C repeats]*. Let that work.

C: *[Falls silent for 30 seconds]* The head has become hollow and transparent. The pressure in my lower neck has become stronger on the right side.

W: Okay. I remove all non-me energy *[C repeats]* in connection with this hollow, angry head *[C repeats]* from all my cells, from my body and from my personal space *[C repeats]* and I send it to where it truly belongs *[C repeats]*.

C: *[Falls silent for 20 seconds]* The head has become a white balloon that hangs from a string. The pressure is the same as before.

W: Okay. I retrieve all my energy *[C repeats]* bound up in all my reactions to this hollow, angry head and this white balloon, hanging from a string, *[C repeats]* and take it back to the right place in my Self *[C repeats]*.

C: *[Falls silent for 30 seconds]* I'm having a thought. I can sense resistance. 'Do I want to be rid of this?' If I stop being lazy then I'll have to work.

W: If I stop being lazy then I'll have to work?

C: I quite often say: 'I'm not just about work.' Work isn't the meaning of my life.

W: Let's go back to the beginning. You said: 'I procrastinate.'

C: Yes.

W: How's that now? What's your attitude towards getting things done – or not getting them done?

C: It's the same.

W: What's changed since the cycle with the sentences?

C: If I look closely, the anger is cut in half.

W: You're more relaxed in relation to the tasks that have to be accomplished. Is that right?

C: Yes, you could say that.

W: How distressing is the phrase 'Better today than tomorrow' on a scale from 0 to 10?

C: It's a burden, so an 8 or even a 9. There's pressure in my chest right away.

W: I'm hearing a wish for freedom of choice. But you've just said: 'If I stop being lazy then I'll have to work.'

C: [Laughs] There's a general feeling of being torn. On the one hand I want structure, and on the other I want total freedom. It's logically impossibly to have both.

W: It's a problem to have both simultaneously, but you can have them both sequentially.

C: Hmm. Thanks for the input.

W: I want to go back to the phrase: 'I'll have to work.' Where does this 'have to' come from? Who or what says: 'If I stop being lazy then I'll have to work'? There seems to be someone or something condemning you to work.

C: *[Places his hand on the back of his neck]* It fits with this pressure down here in physical terms.

W: Pressure from behind?

C: Yes, it feels like someone's grabbing my head and pushing it to the right with their left hand.

W: How do you know that this means you have to work?

C: It just fits. There's someone or something pushing me from the right.

W: I retrieve all my energy *[C repeats]* bound up in what's pushing me *[C repeats]* and take it back to the right place in my Self *[C repeats]*.

C: *[Falls silent for 30 seconds]* The pushing has reduced somewhat.

W: I remove all non-me energy *[C repeats]* in connection with this pushing *[C repeats]* from all my cells, from my body and from my personal space *[C repeats]* and I send it to where it truly belongs *[C repeats]*.

C: *[Falls silent for 35 seconds]* It's reduced further. *[Points to his neck]* The pressure here is less.

W: Okay. I retrieve all my energy *[C repeats]* bound up in all my reactions to what's pushing me *[C repeats]* and take it back to the right place in my Self *[C repeats]*.

C: *[Falls silent for 45 seconds]* It's even less. It hasn't completely gone, but it's definitely reduced.

Part III | *Logosynthesis live: a glance over my shoulder*   171

W: What effect does 'I'll have to work' have now?

C: It's changed in the direction of a possibility: 'I may work.'

W: You 'may.' Who says that you may? Where does this come from? If you 'may', then there's some authority giving you permission.

C: [Smiles] Yes, there's something behind me.

W: How far away is it?

C: Well, it's creating pressure again in my neck and spine.

W: How do you know that it's allowing you to work?

C: It says so: 'You may work.'

W: I retrieve all my energy [C repeats] bound up in the 'You may' message [C repeats] and take it back to the right place in my Self [C repeats].

C: [Falls silent for 35 seconds] There's less pressure.

W: I remove all non-me energy [C repeats] in connection with this 'You may' message [C repeats] from all my cells, from my body and from my personal space [C repeats] and I send it to where it truly belongs [C repeats].

C: [Falls silent for 30 seconds] It's reduced further.

W: Okay. I retrieve all my energy [C repeats] bound up in all my reactions to this 'You may' message [C repeats] and take it back to the right place in my Self [C repeats].

C: [Falls silent for 45 seconds] A table's appeared in front of me. I'm sitting at the table. Someone's bending over me and saying: 'You may paint here.' I feel as if I don't really want to paint...

W: I retrieve all my energy *[C repeats]* bound up in this table scene *[C repeats]* and take it back to the right place in my Self *[C repeats]*.

C: *[Falls silent for 35 seconds]* Now I can sit up straight at the table.

W: I remove all non-me energy *[C repeats]* in connection with this table scene *[C repeats]* from all my cells, from my body and from my personal space *[C repeats]* and I send it to where it truly belongs *[C repeats]*.

C: *[Falls silent for 30 seconds]* Now I'm alone at the table. The person who bent over me is gone.

W: Okay. I retrieve all my energy *[C repeats]* bound up in all my reactions to this table scene *[C repeats]* and take it back to the right place in my Self *[C repeats]*.

C: *[Falls silent for 20 seconds]* I now see the table from further away. I don't know if I'm still sitting at it.

W: What happens with the phrase: 'You may paint here'?

C: I react negatively. It's nice of you to say that I may paint, but I decide whether I may paint or not.

W: What happens with: 'I may work'?

C: It has an affirmative quality. Yes, I may work if I want to.

W: What happens with: 'I have to work'?

C: I don't have to work.

W: What happens when you imagine that there are important things to get done?

C: *[Thinks for a long time]* I see myself as active. I sit down and take care of things.

W: What happens if you think 'I'm lazy,' or 'I'm a lazy bum'?

C: I still feel some pressure in my chest. It's a 4 or a 5.

W: What causes this pressure?

C: It's something on my left. There's someone there, touching me on my upper arm and applying pressure. The person is leaning against me a little.

W: How do you react to the pressure?

C: With an inner resistance… I don't like the pressure.

W: What's underneath this resistance?

C: I feel robbed of my freedom. Other people are determining my actions.

W: And how does it feel to be determined by others?

C: Shit.

W: And what's underneath this?

C: How do you mean?

W: I notice that you're resisting. I suspect that you're resisting so that you don't feel whatever lies underneath. I imagine it's very sad for a child if other people don't see what you need. You feel abandoned.

C: Now I'm feeling this…sadness.

W: The resistance is the avoidance of the sadness underneath… What happens when I say this?

C: It makes sense…and sadness comes…along with a feeling of being overwhelmed…

My intuition tells me that Claudio's sadness is the result of a tension that exists between his actual parents and an ideal set of parents that are imagined in his subconscious. I introduce a cycle of Logosynthesis sentences to neutralise the hidden comparison.

W: I'll give you a sentence. I retrieve all my energy *[C repeats]* bound up in the wish to have other parents *[C repeats]* and take it back to the right place in my Self *[C repeats]*.

C: *[Falls silent for 20 seconds]* This calms me.

W: I remove all non-me energy *[C repeats]* in connection with this wish to have other parents *[C repeats]* from all my cells, from my body and from my personal space *[C repeats]* and I send it to where it truly belongs *[C repeats]*.

C: *[Falls silent for 30 seconds]* Hmm.

W: Okay. I retrieve all my energy *[C repeats]* bound up in all my reactions to this unfulfilled wish of having different parents *[C repeats]* and take it back to the right place in my Self *[C repeats]*.

C: *[Falls silent for 25 seconds]* I can see a baby's pram. It's wicker and oval. I'm lying in it on my stomach with my head turned to the left *[laughs]*.

W: I retrieve all my energy *[C repeats]* bound up in this child in the pram *[C repeats]* and take it back to the right place in my Self *[C repeats]*.

C: *[Falls silent for 40 seconds]* The image is disappearing.

W: How do you now react to the phrases 'I'm lazy,' or 'I'm a lazy bum'?

C: They're phrases.

W: Do they apply to you?

C: No, I no longer have any connection to the phrases.

W: How do you react to the phrase you started with: 'I procrastinate'? Is it still valid?

C: It's not about me. I don't put things off; I just do them.

W: Should we end here?

C: *[Laughs with a wide smile on his face]* Yes, I think we'll leave it at that. Thanks.

22 Eric: fear of surgery

ERIC IS A TRAINEE ON A COURSE AT THE INSTITUTE FOR LOGO-SYNTHESIS. I speak with him during a break in a seminar. He tells me that he's very afraid of an upcoming operation, so I offer to help him as part of the seminar. The demonstration lasts for about 20 minutes.

W: Why are you having the operation?

E: I went skiing at Christmas and had an accident. I fell down during a run and immediately felt pain at the top of my left arm. It wasn't bad and I thought that it'd go away. I went to a doctor when it was still sore some two or three weeks later. An MRI scan revealed that several ligaments had been torn and separated, so I needed an operation. I explained the situation to some of my colleagues, and they encouraged me to get a second opinion from a specialist just to be sure. The specialist told me that the ligaments weren't actually separated but were massively torn – two by more than 70%. He also said that my shoulder capsule and a synovial bursa had been damaged. The injuries could be treated with physiotherapy instead of an operation, but I'd always have trouble with the shoulder if I chose this option. I went on holiday with my family a few weeks later and was in constant pain. I decided to have the operation.

The operation is scheduled for a week on Monday. I don't know whether I really want the surgery; it might just be simpler to live with the minor handicap. The first issue is the inconvenience. I wouldn't be able to move my arm at all for the first six weeks, and rehabilitation could take up to six months. All of this trouble would affect my professional life. The second issue is the fear. I've never had a general anaesthetic since childhood and I don't like giving up control. My wife and other people say: 'You'll just fall asleep and then wake up with nothing in between.' I can't get past this 'nothing.' There's going to be pain after the operation but I'm not afraid of this because I know what pain is. I'm afraid of the anaesthesia.

W: I suggest we address the anaesthesia in this demonstration. What do you know about Logosynthesis?

E: Next to nothing.

W: Then I'll briefly explain the procedure. I'll work with you using three sentences. These sentences will be based on what you've just told me. I'll say the sentences and you'll repeat them after me. Something will then happen. I don't know what this something will be; I just say the sentences and you repeat them and allow them to work. Allowing them to work can take anywhere from half a minute to several minutes. People usually change their perceptions of distressing topics once a Logosynthesis cycle is complete.

E: I'm ready.

The introductory phase lasts for around seven minutes. Eric has already worked with me as part of his training at the Institute, so I'm able to build on an existing working relationship.

W: Okay. You've said that control and general anaesthetic are issues for you. Are there other important keywords in your perception of what you're dealing with? You've already mentioned fear as well.

E: Loneliness.

W: What do you mean by 'loneliness'?

E: I've had a new job for the last six months and I have around 30% more work than I can handle. The operation will stop all of that work and I'll be by myself in a single hospital room in a strange environment. I'll also be away from my family.

W: So the keywords are control, general anaesthetic, fear, and loneliness. Which word is the most loaded and causes you the greatest burden?

E: Fear.

W: So you have a fantasy about something and you react to this fantasy with fear. What's the worst that could happen when you think about the general anaesthetic or the loneliness? What images, fantasies, and ideas emerge?

E: *[Hesitates]* The worst that could happen with the general anaesthetic is that the situation could be exploited. I know of cases in which medical professionals aren't always careful with anaesthetised patients.

W: What would you consider to be the worst form of exploitation?

E: People making jokes about movements that I made. Abuse.

W: How distressing is this idea of abuse on a scale from 0 to 10?

E: It's an 8 or a 9.

W: Okay. I'll give you a sentence in parts and you repeat these parts: I retrieve all my energy *[E repeats]* bound up in this fantasy that I could be exploited *[E repeats]* and take it back to the right place in my Self *[E repeats]*. Let the sentence work. You don't need to think about it… Just close your eyes and notice what's happening within yourself.

E: *[Falls silent for 30 seconds and then pulls a face]*

W: What's going on?

E: *[Laughs]* I'm salivating.

W: *[Laughs]* Interesting.

E: I initially felt a pressure in my stomach, but now the pressure has moved upwards.

W: I'll give you a second sentence to repeat: I remove all non-me energy *[E repeats]* connected to this fantasy of being exploited under general anaesthetic *[E repeats]* from all my cells, from my body and from my personal space *[E repeats]* and I send it to where it truly belongs *[E repeats]*. Let this sentence work as well.

E: *[Falls silent for 30 seconds]* And goodbye! I felt that right away.

W: Okay, time for the third sentence. I retrieve all my energy *[E repeats]* bound up in all my reactions to this fantasy of being exploited under general anaesthetic *[E repeats]* and take it back to the right place in my Self *[E repeats]*. Now let that work.

E: *[Falls silent for 25 seconds and then points at his legs]* I feel as if my legs are fat. I won't fall over, that's for certain *[laughs]*.

W: How distressing is the fantasy now? How distressed do you feel on a scale from 0 to 10 when you think about jokes that could be made about your body or how you might be exploited or abused?

E: 3 or 4. More like 3.

W: How do you feel about the operation now that your distress is a 3 or 4?

E: *[Laughs]* They should go ahead and do it!

W: You'd never know if you were exploited or abused anyway.

E: Yes, exactly! *[The group laughs]* Yes, I can let go. I sense that clearly.

W: What about the fear? That's where we started.

E: It's reduced. It's centred on my heart at the moment.

W: This means that your body is reacting to something. Can you explore what this something is? What ideas or images give you the feeling around your heart?

E: Control happens on a cognitive level for me. I can now let go of the cognitive level and relax in myself without fearing a breakdown.

Eric's answer confused me. I had suspected that there was another, deeper layer that still needed work. But there was no fantasy any more; Eric had already switched over to reflection. The process had advanced further than I'd anticipated.

W: Imagine going in for the operation a week on Monday. What happens?

E: I'll think of you! *[Laughs]* What's different? I'm more relaxed and I'll be able to let go more easily.

W: And what happens when you imagine lying in the single hospital room after the operation? How's that?

E: *[Laughs]* I'll just lie there! I've always said that I'll commit to healing as quickly as possible. I feel this now as well.

W: Is loneliness still an important issue?

E: No, because I'm now occupied with how I can work on myself. I'll let go and focus on healing.

W: Okay. Can we stop here or is something else making you anxious? I'll repeat the four keywords from before: general anaesthetic, control, fear, and loneliness.

E: No, I feel relaxed. But I do want to say something: I'd be afraid of you right now if I didn't already know you! *[Laughs]* I'm not yet familiar with Logosynthesis but it's unbelievable how quickly it works. It's fantastic.

Eric writes to me a year after the operation to tell me that everything had gone well. He hadn't been afraid of the operation after our session and he had taken an interest in everyone around him until the anaesthetic did its work. He had woken up from the procedure in a great mood and soon became busy with his recovery. Patients can't normally work for six weeks after the operation, but Eric was back in the office after only three weeks. He was 95% healed after six months, and the remaining 5% followed within a year.

23 Esther: longing for contact

ESTHER IS A COACH AND THE MOTHER OF THREE CHILDREN. She took a trip to South America with her husband last year and her mother cared for her two sons, aged 14 and 16, while they were away. The boys and their grandmother had a difficult time together, and there's now been no contact between the family and the grandmother for the past six months.

Esther's 29 year-old daughter recently said that she would like to re-establish contact; she would feel terrible guilt if something happened to her grandmother before contact had been restored. This argument is enough for Esther to try and make peace with her mother.

Our Logosynthesis session takes place via Skype and lasts for 30 minutes. The first 9 minutes are spent with Esther explaining the situation.

W: You've described the situation between your mother and your children. What's your goal?

E: To make peace with my mother. I'm always afraid that something could happen and I wouldn't have her anymore… And not talking to her for 20 years isn't a nice idea, either.

W: You have this wish and you don't know if it can be fulfilled. You have energy bound up in this wish. In the end your mother will make her own decision just as you'll make your own decision.

E: Correct.

W: It seems like damage was done and she feels quite insulted.

E: She must have been really insulted when she separated from my biological father. She was always aggressive and combative, even with us children.

W: People become aggressive when they're not seen and/or not taken seriously. Beneath aggression is always abandonment. Did she live through the Second World War?

E: Yes. The family had to flee Bohemia when the war ended. She lost her brother in the war. She also had a heart problem and a condition that made her limp. She had these medical issues since the first grade. There were lots of reasons for her to develop aggression.

W: For you it's now a question of finding a way out – identifying how to clear everything on your side while leaving your mother to face her responsibilities and fate.

E: Exactly.

I had enough information to be able to work with Logosynthesis, but I first decided to set Esther's relationship with her mother in a wider context. This would help her to consider another perspective.

W: It sounds like a difficult fate. There's a lot of abandonment there. You also said that your sons didn't take your mother seriously during their stay – and that she responds with aggression when this happens.

E: Yes.

W: I want to start with your wish itself. Lots of energy can be bound up if a wish and reality are far apart. What happens when you think about your wish of making peace with your mother?

E: The first image that I see is of me standing opposite her and talking to her again *[she sighs]*.

W: What's happening now? Why did you sigh?

E: Such heaviness… My jaw hurts and my throat is starting to close up.

W: This is a reaction to the image of your mother.

Esther has condensed her wish into an image of her mother (meta-question B) and is experiencing intense physical reactions to this image (meta-question A). No further differentiation is required because we have a strong working relationship and she can perceive her emotions and physical sensations. This was sufficient preparation for the Logosynthesis sentences.

W: Okay. I'll give you a sentence and you repeat it: I retrieve all my energy *[E repeats]* bound up in this image of my mother in which I'm standing across from her *[E repeats]* and take it back to the right place in my Self *[E repeats]*.

E: *[Closes her eyes and falls silent for four minutes. She then looks at me.]*

W: What's happening?

E: *[Points to the left]* I noticed something pulling my head in that direction. Then my head went back *[breathes deeply]* as energy was released. Now there's a light lump in my throat *[points at her throat]*. There's stillness in my head.

W: Then I have the next sentence for you: I remove all non-me energy *[E repeats]* in connection with this image of my mother in which I'm standing across from her *[E repeats]* from all my cells, from my body and from my personal space *[E repeats]* and I send it to where it truly belongs *[E repeats]*.

E: *[Falls silent for a minute. She then breathes deeply and her eyes move rapidly. She remains silent for another two minutes before breathing deeply again.]*

W: What's happening?

E: My head was pulled to one side again. I had the feeling of being able to breathe quite deeply. I also tried to move my head faster, but that didn't work. I can feel a slight pressure in my lower jaw…

W: Then here's the third sentence: I retrieve all my energy *[E repeats]* bound up in all my reactions to this image of my mother in which I'm standing across from her *[E repeats]* and take it back to the right place in my Self *[E repeats]*.

E: Now it's as if the energy went out through my ear but is tickling me inside. I also feel that energies are moving in my left arm…

W: Drink a glass of water.

E: *[Stands up, gets water, and drinks]* I needed that.

W: That's part of the process. You should drink water as soon as you feel dizzy or as if energy isn't flowing properly.

E: *[Breathes deeply for one minute and then looks at me clearly]* There's calm in my head.

W: What happens when you think of the image of the mother you would have liked to have had?

E: It isn't important.

W: What isn't important?

E: Standing across from her. It's as if I feel indifference.

W: Indifference or relaxation?

E: When I imagine standing across from her I feel… No, I don't feel anything. I'm just standing there.

The process is complete; Esther's unfulfilled wish no longer generates any physical or emotional reactions. I switch to the integration phase.

W: You no longer have the physical reaction from before.

E: No, the thing in my throat isn't there anymore.

W: How does this change your attitude towards your mother and your daughter who wants to re-establish contact?

E: *[Soberly]* It isn't important for me to re-establish contact with my mother at the moment. My daughter can do it if she wants. If my mother wants to make contact with me then she can do this as well, but there's no urgency on my end.

W: What about her upcoming birthday?

E: I'll send her a card. I might even visit her. It's not important at the moment.

W: Is this what you wanted to achieve?

E: Yes; in my head I've restored peace with my mother. It's lovely! *[Laughs]*

W: This means that you don't have to do anything now, correct?

E: Progress will come without me having to show up at my mother's house. If I want to do that then it'll happen by itself. I don't need to force anything. I find it lovely to just be part of the flow of events. Thank you!

Esther has re-established contact with her adult competence and can gauge the situation well. She's reached her goal with just a single Logosynthesis cycle.

24 Francis: overcoming guilt

RANCIS IS A COUNSELLOR WHO'S QUITE EXPERIENCED WITH LOGOSYNTHESIS. She's 55 years old and has been with her current partner for 37 years. They've been married for the last 30 years, but the marriage is now in crisis. Francis had an affair 20 years ago with her boss at that time. Her husband found out and has suffered from regular bouts of depression ever since, but the marriage continued. They just carried on, building a business together and raising their son. Everything was swept under the carpet.

Francis comes to see me because she can't escape feelings of guilt about the affair. Our session takes place via Skype and lasts for around 30 minutes. It includes two Logosynthesis cycles of three sentences.

F: A few weeks ago I told my husband that we were reaching a breaking point. He seemed depressed and replied: 'I just can't get out of my own skin.' I always confront him right away when he feels like this. I wanted to know what was bothering him and he said: 'I just can't forgive and forget.' I felt strange and didn't know what to do. Separation seemed like a possibility but it didn't feel like a solution. Now everything's up in the air and I feel as guilty as ever.

W: You're in a relationship in which your husband feels blocked because of an event. You weren't previously aware of the large role that the event has been playing in his life. What's your goal for this session?

F: *[Agitated]* I'd like to overcome this profound guilt that's weighing on me. I've ruined this person's whole life, but I want to look at the issue soberly and say: 'Okay, it happened. There's no way around that.' These last couple of months outweigh all the good that we've shared over the last 20 years. It's as if the last 20 years don't count, as if the child we've raised and what we've built together isn't important. I want to be able to think normally and consider the affair's actual consequences for me – without the constant guilt.

W: If I understand you correctly, you're looking for an attitude similar to: 'This is life. These things happen and nobody gets off easily. My husband has a problem but it doesn't have to be my problem.'

F: Exactly. And I want to leave the decisions to him. I like to talk and be rational; he has to come to terms with what happened, and if he needs help then he has to find it. I can't do these things for him.

W: Guilt means that something should have been different or would have had to be different. You wouldn't be guilty if the affair hadn't happened.

F: I have a guilty conscience. I worked on it with my training supervisor and came to the conclusion: 'It's in the past.' But apparently it's not over. The breach of trust is too great for my husband. He's still with me, but I don't want to face a constant guilty conscience if I stay with him.

I now know Francis' situation, her pain, and her desired results from the session. I don't find it necessary for her to describe her pain in further detail. Francis is in firm contact with her emotions and I proceed on the assumption that she can notice changes by herself. I continue with meta-question B.

W: How should your husband be?

F: *[Laughs]* He should talk about the problem or get help. If he can't do either of these things then he should try to forgive me. Then I'd feel better.

W: Okay. Imagine this ideal husband. What do you perceive when you think of him? Do you see him? Hear him?

F: Of course I can see that he's hurt. I don't want to argue about that. But I see a man who says that we could and can get through this. He tries to forgive me, and if he can't manage this, he asks me to show understanding. That would be a partnership.

W: *[Recognises that F is answering in metaphorical instead of concrete terms]* Where do you perceive this man in space?

F: *[Points to her left]* He's standing to my left.

W: How far away is he?

F: One metre.

W: How do you perceive him? Do you see him? Hear him?

F: I see him clearly. He's very strong and very present. That's interesting; it's quite different from how I normally perceive my husband.

Meta-question B creates a clear image of Francis' wished-for husband. We're now ready to apply the three sentences.

W: I'll give you a sentence that you'll repeat in parts: I retrieve all my energy *[F repeats]* bound up in this image of my husband *[F repeats]* and take it back to the right place in my Self *[F repeats]*.

F: *[Falls silent]*

W: *[Applies an ideomotor cue to check whether the process is complete – see Chapter 13. He breaks the silence after two minutes.]* What's going on?

F: First there was sadness, but then I felt strength within myself. *[Breathes deeply]* Then I thought that I should perhaps forgive myself for what I did. The image of my husband is now much smaller and further away.

W: Okay, then I'll give you another sentence: I remove all non-me energy *[F repeats]* in connection with this image of my husband *[F repeats]* from all my cells, from my body and from my personal space *[F repeats]* and I send it to where it truly belongs *[F repeats]*.

F: *[Falls silent for two minutes. She then makes eye contact.]*

W: What's happening?

F: Sadness was there very briefly, but it's now disappeared. An unbelievable pressure in my shoulders is also gone, replaced by an enormous relief *[breathes deeply]*.

W: I retrieve all my energy *[F repeats]* bound up in all my reactions to this image of my husband *[F repeats]* and take it back to the right place in my Self *[F repeats]*. Let that work…

F: *[Falls silent for a minute. She then makes eye contact.]*

W: Okay, what's happening now?

F: I feel as if I don't have to react when he has issues. I don't have to make dramas out of the issues. I can leave them up to him.

W: You said before that: 'I should perhaps forgive myself for what I did.' How's that now?

F: I don't really have to forgive myself at all. It just happened and it's in the past. I no longer feel guilty. I don't have to live by *mea culpa, mea culpa, mea maxima culpa* any more and so create hell for myself.

Ideals always lead to reactions of inferiority. Francis dissolved the image of an ideal husband in just a single cycle of three sentences. Her inferiority reaction to this image – the feeling of guilt – disappeared along with it. But I get the impression that she's not entirely sure of herself. There seems to be a disparaging part that's active in the background and that wants to send her to hell. I continue by exploring the wider topic of guilt, hoping to help her process the distressing experiences that I suspect are present.

W: Guilt is often connected with values, rules, and norms that you've been taught. Where do your values, rules, and norms come from?

F: Ten years at boarding school in a Catholic convent *[breathes heavily and pulls a face]*.

W: What's happening?

F: *[Laughs in a strained way]* I'm just seeing the nuns. We constantly had to go to confession. Even a single bad thought had to be confessed. That's bad.

W: You see the nuns?

F: Yes.

W: Where are the nuns? Left, right, in front, behind?

F: They're standing behind me, threateningly.

W: Do you see them? Hear them?

F: I feel them. I sense the anger that they always had towards us. We had to be good children.

Meta-question B is answered; Francis kinaesthetically senses the energy structure of the nuns behind her in her personal space.

W: How distressing is the nuns' presence on a scale from 0 to 10?

F: An 8.

W: I retrieve all my energy *[F repeats]* bound up in these nuns behind me *[F repeats]* and take it back to the right place in my Self *[F repeats]*.

F: *[Exhales sharply]*

W: What's going on?

F: That was harder. I'm hanging on firmly. They still have quite a lot of power.

I don't go into intense emotions that emerge. Normal, empathetic intervention might dull the image of the nuns, but I want to dissolve it. The second Logosynthesis sentence proves to be much more effective.

W: I remove all non-me energy *[F repeats]* in connection with these nuns behind me *[F repeats]* from all my cells, from my body and from my personal space *[F repeats]* and I send it to where it truly belongs *[F repeats]*.

F: *[Falls silent for a minute and then breathes deeply]* That was good. They're now much further back. I don't feel them any more.

W: Okay. I retrieve all my energy *[F repeats but says 'energies'; I let her correct herself]* bound up in all my reactions to the nuns behind me *[F repeats]* and take it back to the right place in my Self *[F repeats]*.

F: *[Falls silent for a minute and then begins to laugh]* I'm not going to hell! My goodness! Thank you.

W: How old are you?

F: 55.

W: And you've had to live for so long before you could let go of the nuns behind you… *[laughs as well]*

F: They were deeply dug in!

Francis has now neutralised the image of the nuns, so further questioning about her burden from the scene is unnecessary. The Logosynthesis part of our session lasted for around 15 minutes. I continue by discussing the nuns and their educational methods so as to aid Francis' cognitive integration. Her sister is also an issue; she's depressed and suffered from the same strict education. I finish by returning to Francis' original feelings of guilt.

W: You started the session by sharing your wish to take a rational look at the feelings of guilt that you experienced. How is this now?

F: There's no more guilt.

W: How will you go forwards with all this?

F: I'll go forwards in the knowledge that I have no guilt. I'll give my husband the time and space that he needs to work through the issues by himself and in his own way. I don't have to stay silent, but I also don't have to do anything. If he wants to talk then I'm open to that… I honestly have to say that I now feel completely different.

Our conversation ends with a colleague-to-colleague consideration of how Logosynthesis was used in the session. I find it important for clients to be in 'adult' mode when sessions come to a close.

Francis writes to me a few days later: 'Nothing has changed outwardly but the guilt is gone and I've kept a neutral perspective. I can leave him to himself. I feel unbelievably relieved!'

I receive another message after several weeks: 'I decided to write my husband a letter 10 days after our session. I explained that I was writing because my temper might flare up if we talked. I told him that I wouldn't feel guilty for something that had happened 20 years ago and that he should look for help if he couldn't move on. He took me in his arms the next morning and apologised!!! He had never done this before. He said that he was sorry and that he was certain he could now forget about the affair. Four weeks have passed and he's loving, accessible, talks more, and is becoming more and more the man I married 30 years ago.'

25 Geraldine: scenes on the battlefield

G ERALDINE IS A 37 YEAR-OLD BUSINESSWOMAN WHO'S IN THE PROCESS OF ESTABLISHING HERSELF AS A COACH. She's currently participating in a coaching training programme at the Institute for Logosynthesis. In the 'Path of the Will' seminar she expresses a wish to work as a coach in the uppermost levels of organisations. She also notices a feeling of pressure whenever she thinks about this goal. Our session lasts for 18 minutes.

G: I was talking to one of my colleagues about my goals a while back. She said: 'Aren't the other people good enough for you? Do you need to inflate your ego by mixing with people at the leadership level?' This idea causes me stress, but maybe it's true! Perhaps I want to work with leaders because it's cool, sounds good, and maybe offers more money.

W: Let's turn it around: what would happen if you couldn't coach at the highest levels?

G: The degree of effectiveness would be less. More people benefit when an organisation's leadership is content. I could coach at the lower levels and the value for individuals would be the same, but the overall effect would be less if you looked at the organisation as a whole.

W: So you believe that lots of people need to benefit from you?

G: *[Shaken but defiant]* Yes.

W: *[Pauses for a moment]* Say aloud that you want many people to benefit from you.

G: I want many people to benefit from me.

W: What happens in reaction to the sentence?

G: It's unpleasant. I'm stressed.

Geraldine's wish to work at the highest levels doesn't seem to be a task from Essence. She wouldn't react with stress if this were the case. I ask meta-question A to clarify the suffering.

W: How do you notice the stress?

G: I think: 'No, no way.'

W: That's a thought. What kind of emotions do you experience?

G: Fear.

W: What kind of physical sensations are there?

G: Pressure on my shoulders, tension… Also tightness in my chest… My heart pounds…

W: How great is the burden of these emotions and physical sensations when they're combined with the 'No, no way' thought?

G: My initial response is to say '2', but somehow this doesn't fit.

The second order dissociation is still active but the defences are weakening.

W: Explore the emotions, physical sensations, and 'No, no way' thought further. How distressing are they on a scale from 0 to 10?

G: Now it's a 9.

W: So 'I want many people to benefit from me' brings you to a 9 on the 0 to 10 distress level. *[Pauses for a moment]* I assume that something that burdens you in this way isn't Essence.

G: *[Somewhat rebelliously]* Hmm…

I've identified Geraldine's suffering clearly enough for the later reassessment stage. I now move on to meta-question B. I work with the belief as an energy construct and don't refer to its archaic roots.

W: Where is the 'I want many people to benefit from me' sentence in your space?

G: It's in the back of my neck.

W: How do you know that it's there? Do you see it? Hear it?

G: It's more like a pressure.

Geraldine is aware of the reaction but not the trigger. Further clarification is needed.

W: That sounds like a reaction. You can either see or hear the sentence's content. You can react to the content with pressure, but I'd like to separate the reaction from the trigger. So where is the sentence in space? In your body? Outside it? To the left or right? Above or below? In front or behind? Where do you see or hear it?

G: I'm in a distorted film. It's like there are scenes that are playing behind me. There are black horses. *[Laughs]* It's a whole scene that's playing out.

W: *[Confused as to whether the scene is relevant to the issue]* Would you suffer if the scene wasn't there?

She can't answer my rational question. The experience is too intense to be avoided by rational means.

G: I can't get rid of it. It's seems like I'm on a battlefield.

W: I retrieve all my energy *[G repeats]* bound up in these black horses and the battlefield *[G repeats]* and take it back to the right place in my Self *[G repeats]*.

G: *[The image develops further after 10 seconds. G laughs incredulously and seems excited.]* I see myself there with a lance. 'We have to get through!'

W: *[Gives a new first sentence]* I retrieve all my energy *[G repeats]* bound up in this image with the lance *[G repeats]* and take it back to the right place in my Self *[G repeats]*.

G: *[Falls silent for 15 seconds]* Now there are many corpses in front of me.

W: *[Gives another first sentence]* I retrieve all my energy *[G repeats]* bound up in this image of the many corpses *[G repeats]* and take it back to the right place in my Self *[G repeats]*.

G: *[Falls silent for 20 seconds and then speaks calmly]* Now everything's quiet.

W: I remove all non-me energy *[G repeats]* in connection with this scene with the black horses, with the lance, with the corpses, *[G repeats]* from all my cells, from my body and from my personal space *[G repeats]* and I send it to where it truly belongs *[G repeats]*.

G: *[Falls silent for 30 seconds. She then makes eye contact.]* Hmm…

W: I retrieve all my energy *[G repeats]* bound up in all my reactions to this war scene *[G repeats]* and take it back to the right place in my Self *[G repeats]*.

G: *[Falls silent for 20 seconds]* It's gone.

W: Okay. What's going on in your neck now? The 'I want many people to benefit from me' sentence previously caused you a distress level of 9. How is the feeling in your neck – the pressure?

G: It's no longer relevant. I don't feel that many people need to benefit from me.

W: *[Interested]* Ah? So the 'I want many people to benefit from me' sentence is no longer valid?

G: That's right.

W: What's valid now? What do you want now?

G: It doesn't matter who I coach. It's about that person progressing on his or her path.

Geraldine is quite calm and relaxed. She closes the process by talking to me about the consequences of the new insight for her current practice.

The group later discusses the meaning of such historical scenes. Archaic themes like this often surface in Logosynthesis applications, especially when clients work with their issues on a deep level alongside professionals whom they trust. The content of the scenes is often related to violent death and destruction.

It's pointless to philosophise about such phenomena within Logosynthesis' framework. It doesn't matter whether the client is re-experiencing a traumatic event from a past life or has unconsciously constructed the scene as a metaphor for his actual issue. The phenomena may be real to the client, but we regard them as frozen energy structures that stand in the way of the client's full potential. They're represented in three-dimensional space and lead to distressing reactions. They also dissolve when the Logosynthesis sentences are applied to them, thereby allowing the client a more complete experience of the here-and-now.

26 Iris: traces of sexual abuse

IRIS IS A 38 YEAR-OLD PROFESSIONAL. She's married and has a young son. Her father is an alcoholic and has been dependent on her for emotional support since her mother's death. Her brother has schizophrenia.

Iris' recent psychotherapy work has focused on the possibility that her father sexually abused her as a child. The idea has derailed her and she's begun to neglect her son and distance herself from her husband. She thinks 'You filthy pig!' whenever her husband approaches. She's repulsed by her behaviour and doesn't believe that she knows herself any more.

She breaks down into tears shortly after our session begins. She doesn't know if the abuse actually happened and she's torn between revulsion, anger, grief, shame, and love for her father. Our conversation covers the part that she's repressed until now. She's always adapted to meet other people's wishes, and the idea that she can be more than an extension of third-party wishes is new to her. She's only just realising that she can refuse sex and control access to her vagina. The transcript begins at this point and covers the session's final 15 minutes.

I: That triggers it, the word 'vagina.'

W: What triggers the word 'vagina'?

I: *[A long silence]* A penis in it. A penis that I don't want.

No clarification is needed; the traumatic event is fully activated and there's a representation in the form of a penis. I give the first sentence immediately.

W: I retrieve all my energy *[I repeats]* bound up in the representation of the penis that I don't want *[I repeats]* and take it back to the right place in my Self *[I repeats]*.

I: *[Falls silent for around 20 seconds before speaking in a frightened tone]* The thought's there again: 'You filthy pig!'

The process is unfolding rapidly and Iris' reaction to her partner's approach now has a context. Our working relationship is contained within the sentences' structures, so there's no need for any empathetic reaction on my part.

W: I remove all non-me energy *[I repeats]* in connection with this penis that I don't want *[I repeats]* from all my cells, from my body and from my personal space *[I repeats]* and I send it to where it truly belongs *[I repeats]*.

I: *[Falls silent for 30 seconds and then grabs her heart]* Now I feel a weight on my chest.

The process brings an important new sensory perception to the surface – the weight of her father's body. I skip the third Logosynthesis sentence to focus on this new perception.

W: What is the weight?

I: *[Sobbing heavily]* My father's body.

W: I retrieve all my energy *[I repeats]* bound up in the perception of his body *[I repeats]* and take it back to the right place in my Self *[I repeats]*.

I: *[Falls silent for 20 seconds and then breathes deeply]* I feel as if I can breathe again.

W: I remove his energy *[I repeats]* in connection with this perception of his body *[I repeats]* from all my cells, from my body and from my personal space *[I repeats]* and send it to the right place within him *[I repeats]*.

I don't use the words 'non-me energy' in the second sentence because a primary relationship is involved. I instead directly return the father's energy that's stored in the daughter's system.

I: *[Falls silent for 20 seconds. She then drinks a sip of water and suddenly seems quite relaxed]* Yes. That topic again.

W: Okay. I retrieve all my energy *[I repeats]* bound up in all my repeated, practised, and learned reactions to the perception of his body *[I repeats]* and take it back to the right place in my Self *[I repeats]*.

The third sentence is expanded to address the entire spectrum of possible reactions.

I: *[Pauses for 40 seconds before speaking in a balanced tone]* It's funny, but my doubt is lessening. I just had a conversation with my dad in my thoughts. I told him: 'You have your history and you are how you are.' I still don't know if the abuse happened, but my initial doubts have reduced.

I've worked with Logosynthesis for many years, but I still continue to be deeply impressed by the course of such trauma treatments. Important aspects of the traumatic events have been processed within 10 minutes and Iris is now relaxed in the present. Doubts that previously led to despair have given way to an adult perspective. Iris has bridged the enormous gap between the painful reality of the powerless child and the adult woman who loves her father in spite of everything. She's done this in one simple sentence that's even directed at her father: 'You have your history and you are how you are.' But more progress is possible, so I don't stop here.

W: How do you now respond to the word 'vagina' and the phrase 'penis that I don't want'?

I: *[Silent for a while]* Now I see a 'no go' hand motion *[she moves one hand back and forth in front of her chest]*. 'Don't come inside me.'

W: Who is the hand motion for?

I: My husband. I expect him to cross a boundary and I see myself doing the motion *[she repeats the hand motion]*. 'Don't come inside me.'

W: This means that the past is still determining the future… What hasn't been neutralised from the past that leads to such a forceful continuation of the pattern? There's 'vagina' and 'penis that I don't want,' but what hasn't been processed?

I: From behind *[she laughs with shame and embarrassment]*. The whole thing is quite embarrassing. From behind. I feel my father from behind. I feel 'You filthy pig!' again.

W: I retrieve all my energy *[I repeats]* bound up in the perception of my father's penis from behind *[I repeats]* and take it back to the right place in my Self *[I repeats]*.

I: *[Falls silent for 20 seconds]* Now I feel immense shame. I'm ashamed to be here with you discussing these issues.

W: I retrieve all my father's energy *[I repeats]* in connection with this perception of his penis from behind *[I repeats]* and take it back to the right place within him *[I repeats]*.

I: *[Falls silent for 30 seconds]* I feel like a stone. So, so heavy.

W: Drink a glass of water. *[I drinks]* Okay. I retrieve all my energy *[I repeats]* bound up in all my practised and learned reactions to my father's penis from behind *[I repeats]* and take it back to the right place in my Self *[I repeats]*.

I: My heart's pounding and I feel dizzy. I definitely wouldn't have the co-ordination required to thread a needle right now.

W: It sounds as if your system needs reorganising.

I: Now I feel like I did after we processed the shaking trauma *[we'd processed a shaken baby trauma in an earlier session]*. I was shaking then as well.

W: How do you respond to 'from behind' and 'You filthy pig!'?

I: *[Considers the question for several moments]* I need time to let it settle.

W: That sounds like a good idea. We've covered a lot. How do you find thinking about your husband?

I: *[Laughs and smiles brightly]* I love him!

W: And sex with him?

I: It seems fresh to me. I look forward to building something new with him, but right now it's a little too much.

W: I only asked how you found the thought. I didn't say that you should do anything.

I: The idea isn't scary.

W: You don't have to explore that now. Find out with time. It sounds to me like a process has been set in motion. You'll uncover its effects on a daily basis. Do you think that we can end here?

I: *[Glowing]* Yes. Thank you, Willem.

I meet Iris and her husband in a different context several weeks after our session. She thanks me again for our work and it's evident that the couple have found their way back together.

Iris later asks me to include the following statement in this book:

The fascinating thing about the experience is that I came to you because of professional concerns. I was constantly stressed in my job and wanted to know how to find some relief. We never worked on this problem in any of the sessions. We always focused on the sexual abuse that suddenly surfaced. But my professional situation has also relaxed and improved now that the abuse has been dissolved.

PART IV

LIVING LOGOSYNTHESIS: THE PRACTICE

Introduction

THIS SECTION OFFERS IDEAS FOR INTEGRATING LOGOSYNTHESIS INTO YOUR PERSONAL AND PROFESSIONAL LIFE.

Chapter 27 is about Logosynthesis' range: it can be a simple method to add to your list of development tools, or it can be a comprehensive model that aids your understanding of yourself, other people, and the world.

Chapter 28 covers the Logosynthesis training curriculum for coaching, psychological counselling, supervision, and psychotherapy professionals.

Chapter 29 is a glossary of Logosynthesis' most important concepts.

27 Everyday learning

J OHANN SEBASTIAN BACH SAID THAT 'NO MASTER HAS EVER FALLEN FROM HEAVEN.' Roger Federer similarly trained as if he had never won a Masters. It's important to take the same attitude when you apply Logosynthesis, as practice helps you to maintain and build on your current proficiency level.

Several stages of Logosynthesis application have emerged over the past few years. These stages vary from the use of Logosynthesis as a purely technical method to reliance on it for comprehensive insights into the effects and significance of Essence. The speed at which you move through these stages will depend on your level of experience and development, your use of Logosynthesis on yourself, and your application of the model with your clients. Competence with the model grows at every stage – along with the power of Essence.

We can currently identify the following three stages of Logosynthesis application:

- New practitioners use Logosynthesis as an instrument for the relief of pain and suffering. They limit themselves to the technical application of the basic procedure as is taught in Logosynthesis Basic, and they use the sentences within the context of their own frameworks. Many new practitioners refrain from using Logosynthesis with their clients until they've completed more advanced training that allows them to gain further experience and a deeper awareness of the model.

- The next stage sees a shift in focus to awareness of energy flow between Essence and the Self. Acceptance of Logosynthesis' four basic assumptions and their meanings increases, and self-application of the model gains in intensity and clarity. Practitioners learn to understand their clients' experiences not just as psychological phenomena, but also as manifestations of free or bound up energy. Models that were previously known fade into the background.

— Advanced application sees a growing awareness of what living from Essence can mean. Only now do practitioners notice how many of their own thoughts and feelings remain dissociated as frozen reactions to long irrelevant energy structures. Distressing topics in everyday life are recognised more quickly and application of the model shifts to working with topics that were previously unable to emerge, e.g. prenatal or early childhood trauma, life-long patterns, and even direct confrontation with a void of existential abandonment. The deeper the knowledge of one's own processes becomes, the easier and more effective work with clients becomes in turn. This even applies to topics that practitioners found extremely distressing earlier on.

Essence will take the lead with time, removing your dependence on patterns, memories, expectations, fantasies, ideas, wishes, and hopes. Logosynthesis will become a daily exercise for your mental health and personal and spiritual development.

This book can help you to progress through the first stages of Logosynthesis application, but subsequent development is difficult without personal guidance and training. Logosynthesis will inevitably question many patterns that are familiar in your professional life and relationships, and group training offers an excellent space in which to come to terms with this questioning.

28 Logosynthesis training

LOGOSYNTHESIS' POTENTIAL REACHES FAR BEYOND THE SCOPE OF THIS BOOK. The basics of the method are simple to learn, but professional work with clients requires training in coaching, counselling, or psychotherapy as well as further education in Logosynthesis. If you're serious about integrating the model and its methods into your practice, you're welcome to attend formal training programmes that are accredited by the Logosynthesis International Association. You don't have to walk this path alone.

The Logosynthesis International Association

The Logosynthesis International Association sets standards for the content and structure of professional Logosynthesis training programmes. Certification training is offered as a Practitioner, Instructor Master Practitioner, and Trainer in Logosynthesis. The Association also informs the public about Logosynthesis, training programmes, and trained professionals, and maintains the website at www.logosynthesis.net.

Logosynthese and *Logosynthesis* are internationally registered trademarks. Trained professionals enjoy the legal protections that result from these registrations.

Practitioner training

The Practitioner curriculum is directed at professionals who are trained in coaching, supervision, psychological counselling, or psychotherapy. Participants learn the Logosynthesis model and its methods and also explore Logosynthesis' effects on themselves. The seminars involve regular work in small groups, and peer supervision groups run in parallel to the curriculum to support the learning process.

Participants should be prepared for an intense and personal process that gently questions acquired and utilised methods before transferring what's learnt to the participants' practices. Also central to the Practitioner curriculum is the awareness that any client can activate any professional's personal history. The limits of what your clients can achieve will always be determined by your own limits. Your development and the unfolding of Essence in a professional context are therefore key goals of the programme – just as in the Instructor and Master Practitioner programmes.

The following elements are included in the curriculum:

Logosynthesis Basic seminar

This introductory seminar acquaints you with the model, the basic approach, and the method with the help of theoretical lectures, demonstrations, group discussions, and lots of exercises. The content covers Logosynthesis' view of the human person, the seven aspects of guided change, the four basic assumptions, and the basic Logosynthesis procedure. Video and live demonstrations are followed by your first experiences of Logosynthesis application as a client and as a counsellor.

Logosynthesis Live

This workshop provides an opportunity for you to deepen your knowledge of Logosynthesis through the processing of your own topics. Participants bring their own topics and experience the possibilities of Logosynthesis for themselves and others. A broad spectrum of methods is introduced so that you can acquire an overview of the entire field. Each counselling session is followed by opportunities to discuss your observations, theoretical aspects of the work, and the chosen methods and their indications.

Participation in at least two theme seminars

Theme seminars offer a deep understanding of the possibilities that are available when Logosynthesis is applied to important life areas. Seminars include:

- *The Path of Courage* explores how people have dealt with distressing and traumatic events in their pasts, presents, and futures. Familiarity with and treatment of trauma and fear lie at the centre of this seminar.

- *The Path of the Will* describes dealing with life tasks in both success and failure. An important theme is the dissolution of destructive beliefs and distressing memories in connection with the shaping of one's life.

- *The Path of the Bond* focuses on mastering intimacy and distance and the creation and dissolution of relationships. You learn to identify and neutralise destructive everyday patterns in relationships with the help of your own experience and that of other seminar attendees.

Practitioner training is completed with two units of supervision and a written paper on both your personal development and the application of Logosynthesis with a client.

The Practitioner curriculum contains a total of 12 course days and two supervision units (at the date of this book's publication). Supervision units are conducted individually or in groups. You can sign up for all elements of the curriculum separately, but the training always begins with Logosynthesis Basic. You can determine the order of the other elements and select your theme seminars to fit with your interests and area of specialty.

A brochure, training dates, list of trained professionals, and other helpful materials can be found at the website, www.logosynthesis.net. The website also includes information about the curricula for the higher certification levels.

Practitioners report their experiences

Sigrid Stilp, *Trainer, Coach*

I became infected with the Logosynthesis virus right with my first workshop in Lower Austria. I've been working with the sentences ever since, finding my way ever closer to my true Self. When I first heard about the Practitioner course I assumed it was a clever marketing move – but when I finally signed up I was surprised to find out how Logosynthesis is so much more than just a method with three sentences. My consciousness of and gratitude for Logosynthesis grew with every workshop that I attended. I now know that I grow in all of Willem's workshops; there's always something new to experience and learn. I extend my heartfelt thanks to you, Willem. You enrich my life, and my work with Logosynthesis allows me to grow as a person, a supervisor, a trainer, and a coach. I look forward to what's to come.

Dr. Sibylle Honnef, *Management consultant, Coach*

I do a lot of work with Logosynthesis. What you've developed is genius! I've just had a session and applied Logosynthesis again; there are so many old energy structures that can be neutralised with the model. Every time is like a miracle.

Yesterday I completed a process with a client who was in therapy for years and is now seeking help again in her job. She landed on her old topics right away, and in just five sessions I could help to free her from these topics to the extent that she claimed to have never before felt so good. She could hardly believe it, but she 'believed because she experienced.' Someone put it all so nicely: 'Whoever heals is right – or the result makes us right.'

Ulrike Scheuermann, *Author, Psychologist, Coach*

Logosynthesis works, and it works fast. Distressing memories, fantasies, and feelings can often be neutralised in minutes. This speed affects me in my coaching because the results are challenging; it's not easy to accept that development can proceed so quickly. I'm not accustomed to it from other counselling and therapeutic methods. I'm amazed time after time. My clients also learn to accept the method's simplicity and notice its effects in their lives – from spectacular changes to those that are subtler.

And how can you convey the simplicity to others? When people hear about the method but haven't tried it for themselves, they're often quick to label Logosynthesis as a 'miracle method.' It's an interesting challenge to address this quality of simplicity in Logosynthesis' application.

Hans-Georg Hauser, *Trainer in transactional analysis*

How did I ever work without Logosynthesis? This question isn't 100% serious, of course – but it does express my high opinion of what Logosynthesis has brought to my work and way of working. I can't imagine doing what I do as a supervisor, coach, and instructor in transactional analysis, supervision, and coaching without Logosynthesis. It's become an integral element of my work with people. It helps my clients and me to work through and solve difficult situations and it's highly regarded by my trainees and clients alike. All of my trainees and clients learn in their first coaching or supervision sessions that long-standing blocks, hindrances, and limitations can be neutralised so rapidly, simply, and elegantly.

29 Glossary

LOGOSYNTHESIS RELIES ON MANY CONCEPTS THAT ARE MISSING FROM OTHER APPROACHES TO GUIDED CHANGE. This glossary includes definitions for the most important of these concepts. Other concepts that have specific meanings in Logosynthesis are also included.

Activation: see **Trigger**

Application

The application of Logosynthesis helps to free an individual's life energy that's caught in frozen worlds. A stable working relationship is necessary for this application, just as is customary in other models of guided change. The application process consists of three steps:

- The person takes back into himself his own energy that's bound up in an introject or a portion of an introject
- The person removes the energy of other people and objects that's left behind in his personal space
- The person takes back into himself all of his energy that's bound up in his reactions to the introject.

The process begins when specific sentences are said. The person or his coach or therapist creates these sentences based on information from two meta-questions. The first two sentences are formed with information from meta-question B. The third sentence is indirectly formed with information from meta-question A. Precise answers to the meta-questions are prerequisites for accurate application of the Logosynthesis model.

Assimilation

An individual can react freely to images of assimilated persons and objects – unlike to persons and objects that are represented as introjects (which in turn lead to frozen reactions).

Basic assumptions

Logosynthesis proceeds from four basic assumptions. These assumptions form the foundation of the method and are the rationale behind its effectiveness. The point of departure is that we are Essence, i.e. beings beyond time and space.

- Basic assumption 1
  The lack of awareness of our true nature and task in this world leads to suffering.

- Basic assumption 2
  The awareness of our true nature is reduced or hindered by introjection and dissociation (splitting off).

- Basic assumption 3
  Split-off parts and introjects are frozen energy structures in multi-dimensional space – and not just abstract concepts.

- Basic assumption 4
  The power of the word makes the dissolution of frozen structures possible and frees our life energy for the task of our existence.

Belief, Limiting belief

A (limiting) belief hinders an individual's open perception of himself and his environment in the present. It also hinders the free unfolding of his potential. A (limiting) belief can be taken on from important primary relationships – or can arise from a conclusion that's formed in reaction to statements made or behaviours demonstrated within these primary relationships.

The meta-questions are used to assist in the identification of (limiting) beliefs as energy structures in an individual's personal space. The (limiting) beliefs can then be neutralised or dissolved with the help of the Logosynthesis sentences. A (limiting) belief's truth content can be tested with the 'Validity of the negative cognition' scale.

Black hole

The black hole is the most intense experience of first order dissociation. An individual's contact with Essence and other people is completely cut off and he literally experiences himself as being in a 'black hole'. The black hole is described as 'the long dark night of the soul' in mysticism. Neither Essence nor other people can be perceived in this state.

Cycle

A sequence of three Logosynthesis sentences with their working pauses. A reflection phase usually follows a cycle, allowing the processed aspect to be integrated into the client's frame of reference. A session will sometimes contain only one cycle or no cycles at all, but sessions with between five and seven cycles are not uncommon.

Destructive conviction: see Belief, Limiting belief

Dissociation

An individual splits off parts – or 'dissociates' – when he's unable to assimilate a trauma or distressing event because it overwhelms his capabilities or development. His physical, emotional, and cognitive reactions to the trauma or event split off from the flow of life energy, from Essence, and are stored as frozen parts. A representation of the trauma or event is stored as an introject along with the individual's energy or energy from the outside world. Dissociated parts can be activated at any time through similar traumas or events and then lead to similar reactions.

Earth Life System

The Earth Life System is a three-dimension environment in time that the Self, manifested from Essence, shares with other beings. The Earth Life System contains all the elements of experience that the Self requires to fulfil its task within this environment.

Effect mechanism

Logosynthesis' effect mechanism relates to Essence's influence on frozen structures in an individual's body and personal space. This influence is enacted through the power of the word. Basic Assumption 4 states that words have the ability to focus intention. The content of the Logosynthesis sentences determines the direction of this intention, either taking energy back into the Self or removing it from the individual's body or personal space. The shift in energy is accompanied by changes in physical sensations, emotions, and thoughts.

Emotions

Emotions are innate elements of human experience that are directly tied to an individual's perception of his environment and his corresponding accommodation behaviours (e.g. surprise, joy, rage, fear, revulsion, grief).[69] Emotions serve the survival of individuals and social systems by supporting decision-making, the development of values and norms, and the finding of adequate behaviours for interaction with the environment.

Healthy emotions relate to other people or events in the present. Archaic emotions are frozen reactions to people or events in the past. Logosynthesis acts to identify archaic emotions and dissolve them, allowing individuals to react with healthy emotions.

---

[69]Plutchik, Robert (1980), Emotion: Theory, research, and experience: Vol. 1. Theories of emotion, 1, New York: Academic.

Energy structure

The flow of energy can be influenced by distressing events and then frozen in structures. These structures contain perceptions that are stored in an individual's body and personal space. The structures also contain physical, emotional, and cognitive reactions to the perceptions.

Energy construct: see Energy structure

Essence

A human being is a manifestation of a comprehensive Essence that exists beyond time and space. Religious and spiritual traditions call Essence the higher Self, the true Self, or the immortal soul. Logosynthesis borrows the term Essence from Ali Hameed Almaas and uses it as a neutral concept so as to avoid associations with existing religions, spiritual paths, or schools of guided change. Essence can manifest a Self with a body and psyche in the Earth Life System.

Fantasy

A fantasy is an idea about how the world is, how it could/should be, or how it could/should have been. It's distinguished from sensory perceptions and memories, both of which represent the world in the past or present with the help of the senses. Fantasies are generally just as important as sensory perceptions and memories. The reality content of fantasies varies; a plan may include concrete steps to bring about its realisation, while a wish or dream delegates the realisation to other people or elements of the outside world.

Feeling

A feeling can denote an emotion, a fantasy, an intuition, a physical sensation, a kinaesthetic perception, a thought, a hypothesis, or a belief. Clarification is always required when this word is raised in Logosynthesis, as different meanings can lead to different interventions. Professionals may find it worthwhile to go over the different meanings with their clients.

Foreign energy

Foreign energy is the energy of other people, animals, or objects that's found in an individual's body or personal space as part of an introject. Foreign energy can lead to frozen reactions and is removed with the aid of the second Logosynthesis sentence.

Frozen perception

A frozen perception is a portion of a frozen world in which the sensory experiences of a memory are frozen into an energy structure. Frozen perceptions are inseparably linked to frozen reactions. Frozen perceptions are identified with the help of meta-question B and form the topic of the first two Logosynthesis sentences.

Frozen reaction

A frozen reaction is a portion of a frozen world that includes physical, emotional, cognitive, and behavioural aspects. Frozen reactions are always connected to a trigger. The same reactions will always occur if the associated trigger is activated. Logosynthesis is only concerned with reactions that directly or indirectly lead to suffering. These reactions are identified with the help of meta-question A. The problems that clients bring into counselling sessions are generally brought about by frozen reactions.

Frozen world

All introjects are intimately connected to a group of dissociated circumstances as frozen perceptions. Taken together, these form a frozen world. The concept of a frozen world is closely related to Kernberg's object relations in psychological terms, i.e. an image of a primary relationship is inseparable from a certain emotional state. Kernberg's model fails to include energetic components, however. Our life energy is generally bound up in frozen worlds to a significant extent, and it's these frozen worlds that determine our reaction patterns and form our identities.

Idea: see **Fantasy**

Image: see **Representation**

Internalising: see **Introjection**

Introjection

Events can't be processed if they go beyond the scope of an individual's existing frame of reference and the individual receives no processing support. Representations of people and events then become introjects. Introjects contain energy taken from the individual's Self as well as energy from other people or objects that's been left in the individual's personal space.

Introjects, Activation of

Frozen worlds help us to orient ourselves in life; they create stability in our perceptions of ourselves in our environments. Activated introjects explain much of our daily feelings, thoughts, and actions. When an event causes a painful reaction, however, its introject may also be activated in the future and lead to similar painful reactions. The affected individual is only able to trace these reactions in a limited manner. Logosynthesis is applied when an individual suffers because pain-generating introjects are activated on a daily basis and the individual's normal life in society is inhibited as a result.

Life energy

Life energy is the power of growth within nature that causes organisms to develop into higher forms, embryos to become adults, and healthy people to strive after their ideals. This power has different names in various cultures, including *ka*, *physis*, *prana*, *chi*, the *zero point field*, and, in this book, *Essence*. Life energy can be flowing or frozen and can belong to an individual or to people and objects within an individual's environment.

Meta-questions

The two meta-questions, A and B, are Logosynthesis' most important diagnostic tools. After a session's initial contact, information, and contract phases, a professional condenses a client's biographical details into aspects that are relevant to the suffering. Meta-question A focuses on the suffering itself while meta-question B focuses on the suffering's triggers.

Original Self: see **Self**

Personal space

An individual's personal space is a portion of the three-dimensional field in the Earth Life System that the individual experiences as his own. Personal space usually contains the individual's physical body as well as introjects and dissociated parts. Personal space can equally be understood as an extended aura or an energy field.

Processing

The Logosynthesis sentences have been developed for and are addressed to elements of experience such as memories and fantasies. The saying of each sentence is followed by a working pause in which the power of the word neutralises or assimilates the targeted element. Once a sentence's processing is complete, the emotional charge of the targeted element is reduced or has disappeared. The individual can then gauge the experience from an age-appropriate perspective. Traumatic memories lose their potential to cause anxiety or pain in the wake of processing; the individual can now perceive the traumatic events in a proper context.

Representation (or Image)

A representation (or image) is a three-dimensional energy structure in space that's formed of frozen sensory perceptions (i.e. sight, hearing, touch, smell, taste). It can depict a memory, fantasy, or belief. Representations (or images) must be assimilated to become functional.

Self

The Self is a specific manifestation of Essence within the context of the Earth Life System. The Self controls a body with which it perceives the environment and navigates space – along with a brain that processes information from the sensory organs. It also controls a psyche that directs the body and brain in their confrontations with the environment.

Sentences

Three sentences are created for every frozen world based on a client's answers to meta-questions A and B. The grammatical and syntactical forms of these sentences are almost always the same, with the content relating to the representation of a Theme X – a memory, fantasy, or belief.

The sentences are:

1 *I retrieve all my energy bound up in (the representation of Theme X) and take it back to the right place in my Self.*

2 *I remove all non-me energy related to (the representation of Theme X) from all my cells, from my body and from my personal space, and I send it to where it truly belongs.*

3 *I retrieve all my energy bound up in all my reactions to (the representation of Theme X) and take it back to the right place in my Self.*

A fourth sentence is only introduced when the client is fully in the present and the processing of the corresponding experience is complete:

4 *I tune all of my systems to this new awareness.*

Versions of the Logosynthesis sentences in other languages can be found on the Institute for Logosynthesis website.

Splitting off: see Dissociation

Subjective burden scale

The subjective burden scale assesses the burden that an individual feels from a symptom or reaction to a trigger on a scale from 0 to 10. 0 equates to no burden while 10 is the highest possible level of burden. The scale is one of several tools used in meta-question B.

Trauma

A trauma is the consequence of a distressing event that an individual is unable to process. Logosynthesis considers a trauma to consist of a strong connection of frozen perceptions and ideas with physical, emotional, cognitive, and behavioural reactions. A trauma is dissolved through the application of the Logosynthesis sentences to the frozen perceptions and ideas – leading the reactions to disappear.

Trigger

A trigger is an introject that's activated by people or events in an individual's current environment. Triggers take the form of frozen perceptions and inevitably lead to predictable physical, emotional, and cognitive reactions.

Validity of the negative cognition

The validity of a negative cognition can be assessed on a scale from 0 to 10, allowing a client to gauge the experienced truth of a limiting belief. 0 relates to a limiting belief that's entirely false while 10 relates to a limiting belief that's entirely true. The scale is one of several tools used in meta-question A.

Working pause

A working pause follows each Logosynthesis sentence within a Logosynthesis cycle. Working pauses provide space for the power of the word to neutralise or assimilate the targeted memory, fantasy, or belief. Proper preparation should mean that a working pause lasts for around 90 seconds, although both longer and shorter pauses are also possible.

Wish: see Fantasy

Afterword:
I was never alone
along the way

MANY PEOPLE HAVE INSPIRED ME THROUGH THEIR IDEAS, WORK, AND SUPPORT TIME AND TIME AGAIN, EVEN IF THEY DON'T APPEAR IN MY LIST OF CITED WORKS. Many of the names on the following list were mentioned in my first book, and others have since joined them. The Wespi-group with Daniela Achermann, Claudia Hermeking, Ingo Kitzelmann, Fredy Morgenthaler, Romeo Schenk, Sandro Simonett, and Cornelei von Welser has been a continuous source of inspiration throughout my process. Julie Herson from the Iron Mill Institute in Exeter (UK) offered me the chance to teach Logosynthesis in the early stages of its development. Trish North, Nancy Porter-Steele, and Curtis Steele cleared the way for presentation of the model in Canada. Olga and Vladislav Lukin have, along with Bella Levize, made possible seminars in Moscow. Hans-Georg Hauser organised seminars in Austria, and the same was done by Andrea Fredi in Italy, Frits van Kempen and Karin de Smit in the Netherlands, Yves Wauthier-Freymann and Caroline Dubois in Belgium, and Gisela and Karl-Heinz Holtmann-Scheuermann in Germany. Jürg Kesselring supported me with the neuro-scientific aspects of the work. I'm immensely grateful for the inspiration that I've gained from all of these people.

Isaac Newton said: 'I've stood on the shoulders of giants.' I'd like to list a few of the people upon whose shoulders I've stood, although with no suggestion that the list is exhaustive: A.H. Almaas, Roberto Assagioli, Edward Bach, William Baldwin, Richard Bandler, Graham Barnes, Gregory Bateson, Don Beck, Eric Berne, Gregg Braden, Roger Callahan, Deepak Chopra, Petruska Clarkson, Gary Craig, Mary Cox, the 14th Dalai Lama,

Daniel Dana, Charles Darwin, John Diamond, John Diepold, Don Elium, Masaru Emoto, Milton Erickson, Richard Erskine, Pat Esborg, Ronald Fairbairn, Paul Federn, Sander Ferenczi, Tapas Fleming, Viktor Frankl, Sigmund Freud, Eric Fromm, Ernest Galanter, Fred Gallo, Eugene Gendlin, Birger Gooss, David Gordon, Mary & Bob Goulding, Claire Graves, John Grinder, Stanislav Grof, David Grove, Onno van der Hart, David Hawkins, Aldous Huxley, Sandra Ingerman, Pierre Janet, John the Evangelist, Carl Gustav Jung, Arthur Koestler, Bessel van der Kolk, Joseph LeDoux, Howard Lipke, Bruce Lipton, Karen Malik, Abraham Maslow, James Masterson, George Armitage Miller, Charles Samuel Myers, Greg Nicosia, Friedrich Nietzsche, Larry Philip Nims, Eric Pearl, Frederick Perls, Plato, Karl Pribram, Ernest G. Schachter, Rupert Sheldrake, Carl & Stephanie Simonton, Peter Sloterdijk, Socrates, Keely Stahl, Mother Teresa, Edoardo Weiss, Donald Winnicott, Mary 'Mo' Wheeler, Bob Yourell…

Bibliography

Almaas, A. H. (1998). Essence with the Elixir of Enlightenment. The Diamond Approach to Inner Realization. York Beach, Maine: Samuel Weiser, Inc.

Assagioli, R. (1965). Psychosynthesis. A Manual of Principles and Techniques. New York: Hobbs, Dorman.

Bandler, R. & Grinder, J. (1975). The Structure of Magic I: A Book about Language and Therapy. Science and Behavior Books.

Bandler, R. & Grinder, J. (1975). The Structure of Magic II: A Book About Communication and Change. Palo Alto, CA: Science & Behavior Books.

Berne, E. (1961). Transactional Analysis in Psychotherapy. New York: Grove.

Berne, E. (1982). A Layman's Guide to Psychiatry and Psychoanalysis. Simon & Schuster.

Boszormeny-Nagy, I. & Spark, G. (1984). Invisible Loyalties: Reciprocity in Intergenerational Family Therapy. Brunner-Mazel; Reprint edition.

Braden, G. (2007). The Divine Matrix: Bridging Time, Space, Miracles, and Belief. Hay House.

Brazelton, T. B. & Greenspan, S. I. (2001). The Irreducible Needs of Children: What Every Child Must Have to Grow, Learn, and Flourish. Cambridge, MA: Perseus.

Bucay, J. (2013). Let Me Tell You a Story: A New Approach to Healing through the Art of Storytelling. Europa Editions.

Callahan, R. (1985). Five Minute Phobia Cure. Wilmington: Enterprise.

Callahan, R. (2002). Tapping the Healer Within. McGraw-Hill.

Camus, A. (1955). The Myth of Sisyphus. New York: Alfred A. Knopf.

Coelho, P. (1995). The Pilgrimage. New York: Harper-One.

Craig, G. (2011). The EFT Manual. Everyday EFT: Emotional Freedom Techniques Series. Elite Books.

Dawkins, R. (2006). The Selfish Gene. Oxford: Oxford University Press, p. 237.

Diepold J., Jr., V. Britt, S. W. W. Bender(2004). Evolving Thought Field Therapy: The Clinician's Handbook of Diagnosis, Treatment, and Theory. New York: Norton Press.

Emoto, M. (2004). Messages from Water. Hado Kyoikusha.

Feinstein, D. (2012, August 20). Acupoint Stimulation in Treating Psychological Disorders: Evidence of Efficacy. Review of General Psychology. Advance online publication. doi: 10.1037/a0028602.

Feinstein, D. (2008). Energy Psychology: A Review of the Preliminary Evidence. Psychotherapy: Theory, Research, Practice, Training. 45(2).

Ferenczi, S. (1916). Introjection and transference. In his Contributions to psychoanalysis (Ernest Jones, Trans.; pp. 30-80.). Boston: Richard G. Badger. (Original work published 1909).

Frankl, V. (1987). Logotherapie und Existenzanalyse. Texte aus fünf Jahrzehnten. Munich: Piper.

Freud, S. (1960). Briefe 1873-1939, Gesammelte Werke, Bd. 16, Frankfurt a.M., p. 429.

Gallo, F. (2002). Energy Psychology in Psychotherapy. A Comprehensive Source Book. New York, NY: W. W. Norton.

Gallo, F. (2004). Energy Psychology (Innovations in Psychology). CRC Press.

Gendlin, E. T. (1982). Focusing. Second edition. New York: Bantam Books.

Gleick, J. (2012). The Information: A History, A Theory, A Flood. Vintage.

Grinder, J. & Bandler, R. (1981). Trance-Formations: Neuro-Linguistic Programming and the Structure of Hypnosis. Moab, UT: Real People Press.

Grinder, J. & Bandler, R. (1983). Neurolinguistic Programming and the Transformation of Meaning. Moab, UT: Real People Press.

Grinder, J. & Bandler, R. (1996). Patterns of the Hypnotic Techniques of Milton H. Erickson, MD: Volume 1. Metamorphous Press, U.S.

Grof, S. (1998). Human nature and the nature of reality: conceptual challenges from consciousness research. Journal of Psychoactive Drugs. Vol. 30, No. 4.

Van der Hart, O., Steele, K., Boon, S. & Brown, P. (1995). Die Behandlung traumatischer Erinnerungen. Hypnose und Kognition, 12 (2).

Hawkins, D. R. (2005). The Eye of the I: From Which Nothing is Hidden. Veritas Publishing.

Hellinger, B. (2001). Love's Own Truths: Bonding And Balancing In Close Relationships. Zeig, Tucker & Theisen.

Hellinger, B. (2003). Ordnungen des Helfens. Ein Schulungsbuch. Heidelberg: Carl-Auer.

Ingerman, S. (1991). Soul Retrieval: Mending the Fragmented Self. San Francisco: Harper.

James, T. & Woodsmall, W. (1988). Time Line Therapy and the Basis of Personality. Meta Publications.

Janet, P. (1928). L'évolution de la mémoire et la notion du temps. Paris: A. Chahine.

Janet, P. (1928). L'évolution de la personnalité. Paris: A. Chahine.

Kahler, T. (1975). Drivers. The Key tot he Process of Scripts. Transactional Analysis Journal, 5.

Karpman, S. (1968). Fairy Tales and Script Drama Analysis. Transactional Analysis Bulletin, 7 (26).

Lammers, W. & Kircher, B. (2001). The Energy Odyssey. New Directions in Energy Psychology. Maienfeld: ias.

Lammers, W. (2008). Logosynthesis. Change through the Magic of Words. Maienfeld: ias.

Lammers, W. & Fredi, A. (2012). Restoring the Flow – a Primer of Logosynthesis. URL: https://www.smashwords.com/books/view/284465.

Lammers, W. (2015). Self-Coaching with Logosynthesis (CreateSpace).

LeDoux, J. E. (1996). The Emotional Brain. New York, Simon and Schuster.

Van Lommel, P. (2011). Consciousness Beyond Life: The Science of the Near-Death Experience. HarperOne; Reprint edition.

Masaru, E. (1998). Messages from Water. Hado Publishing.

Maslow, Abraham H. (1962). Towards a Psychology of Being. New York: Wiley.

McTaggart, L. (2003). The Field. The Quest fort he Secret Force oft he Universe. Harper.

Milivojevic, Z. (2007). [Games Drug Addicts Play] Novi Sad: Psyhopolis Institute.

Myers, C.S. (1940). Shell shock in France 1914-18. Cambridge, UK. Cambridge University Press.

Nguyen, T. (2012). Psychosynthesis. A Way of Openness. In: International Journal of Psychotherapy, Vol 16 (2).

Nijenhuis, E. R. S. (2004). Somatoform Dissociation: Phenomena, Measurement, and Theoretical Issues. New York: W.W. Norton & Company.

Persinger, M. M. (2001). The neuropsychiatry of paranormal experiences. Neuropsychiatric Practice and Opinion 13 (4).

Pressfield, S. (1995). The Legend of Bagger Vance. New York: Avon.

Putnam, F. (1989). Diagnosis and treatment of multiple personality disorder. New York: Guilford Press.

Radin, D. (2006). Entangled Minds. New York. Paraview Pocket Books.

Shapiro, F. (2001). Eye Movement Desensitization and Reprocessing (EMDR): Basic Principles, Protocols, and Procedures. The Guilford Press.

Sheldrake, R. (2003). The Sense of Being Stared At. London: Random House UK Ltd.

Sloterdijk, P. (2010). Du mußt dein Leben ändern. Suhrkamp Verlag.

Tolle, E. (2004). The Power of Now: A Guide to Spiritual Enlightenment. New World Library.

Truax, C. B. & Carkhuff, R. R. (1967). Towards Effective Counseling and Psychotherapy. Chicago: Aldine.

Varga von Kibéd, M. & Sparrer, I. (2005). Ganz im Gegenteil, Tetralemma-Arbeit und andere Grundformen Systemischer Strukturaufstellungen.

Wilde, O. (1905). De Profundis. URL: http://www.gutenberg.org/ebooks/921. Retrieved 10 December 2012.

Winnicott, D. (1953). Transitional objects and transitional phenomena, International Journal of Psychoanalysis, 34.

Wolpe, J. (1969). The Practice of Behavior Therapy, New York: Pergamon Press.

Yourell, R. (1998). Levels of Consciousness in Psychotherapy. URL: www.psychinnovations.com/levels.html.

Zeh, J. (2009). Schilf. BTB Verlag.

Zellinger, A. (2010). Dance of the Photons. From Einstein to Quantum Teleportation. Macmillan.

About the author

WILLEM LAMMERS, DPSYCH, MSC, TSTA IS A SEASONED SPECIALIST IN THE SUBTLE NUANCES OF MIND, BODY, AND SOUL. He gathered a broad range of experiences as a coach, psychotherapist, trainer, and executive at the VU University in Amsterdam and an alpine clinic in Davos before going on to found *ias*, an institute for the instruction of specialists in guided change. He trained in transactional analysis, hypnotherapy, NLP, and energy psychology and organised Europe's first energy psychology conference in 2001. He has devoted himself to developing and spreading Logosynthesis since 2005. Dr. Lammers now shares his expertise as a coach, psychotherapist, author, seminar leader, speaker, and Logosynthesis trainer, primarily in Europe and North America. This is his sixth book.

238

Disclaimer

THE INFORMATION CONTAINED IN THIS BOOK IS EDUCATIONAL IN NATURE AND IS PROVIDED ONLY AS GENERAL INFORMATION FOR PERSONAL USE. The author accepts no responsibility or liability whatsoever for the use or misuse of the book's information. Please seek professional advice as appropriate before implementing any protocol or opinion expressed in the book and before making any health-related decisions.

Logosynthesis is a relatively new approach and the extent of its effectiveness, benefits, and risks is not fully known. The reader agrees to assume and accept full responsibility for any and all risks associated with reading this book and using Logosynthesis as a result.

The reader understands that if he or she chooses to use Logosynthesis, emotional or physical sensations or additional unresolved memories may surface which could be perceived as negative side effects. Emotional material may also continue to surface after Logosynthesis has been used. This surfacing indicates that other issues may need to be addressed, preferably with the help of a trained professional. Previously vivid or traumatic memories may equally fade when Logosynthesis is used. This fading could adversely impact your ability to provide detailed legal testimony regarding a traumatic incident.

Logosynthesis is not a substitute for medical or psychological treatment. The information presented in this book is not intended to imply the use of Logosynthesis to diagnose, treat, cure, or prevent any disease or psychological disorder. The author makes no warranty, guarantee, or prediction regarding any outcome for using Logosynthesis on any particular issue. The case studies presented in this book similarly do not constitute a warranty, guarantee, or prediction regarding the outcome of an individual's use of Logosynthesis on any particular issue.

You need to become trained and qualified as a Logosynthesis Practitioner in order to use Logosynthesis with others.

While all materials and links to other resources are included in this book in good faith, the accuracy, validity, effectiveness, completeness, or usefulness of any information contained herein, as in any publication, cannot be guaranteed.

If any court of law rules any part of this disclaimer to be invalid, the disclaimer stands as if the invalid parts were struck out. By continuing to read this book you agree to all of the terms above.

66756041R00135

Made in the USA
Middletown, DE
15 March 2018